Twentieth Century
British Drama

John Smart

Series Editor: Adrian Barlow

CAMBRIDGE
UNIVERSITY PRESS

PUBLISHED BY THE PRESS SYNDICATE OF THE UNIVERSITY OF CAMBRIDGE
The Pitt Building, Trumpington Street, Cambridge, United Kingdom

CAMBRIDGE UNIVERSITY PRESS
The Edinburgh Building, Cambridge CB2 2RU, UK
40 West 20th Street, New York, NY 10011–4211, USA
10 Stamford Road, Oakleigh, VIC 3166, Australia
Ruiz de Alarcón 13, 28014 Madrid, Spain
Dock House, The Waterfront, Cape Town 8001, South Africa

http://www.cambridge.org

First published 2001

Printed in the United Kingdom at the University Press, Cambridge

Typefaces: Clearface and Mixage   *System:* QuarkXPress® 4.1

A catalogue record for this book is available from the British Library

ISBN 0 521 79563 X paperback

Prepared for publication by Gill Stacey
Designed by Tattersall Hammarling & Silk
Cover photograph: Photostage/Donald Cooper. Still from *Look Back in Anger*, Lyttleton Theatre 15.7.99 (Jason Hughes, Michael Sheen, Emma Fielding)

Contents

Introduction

The aim of this book is to relate 20th-century British drama to its historical, cultural and social contexts. It is not implied that plays emerge naturally to mirror the society from which they spring, but rather that an understanding of context enhances the understanding and enjoyment of drama.

Looking back on 20th-century British drama from the perspective of this century involves gains and losses. The loss is that it is often hard to understand 'the shock of the new' when it has become absorbed in our own dramatic traditions and expectations. It is hard to recapture that moment when a radically new and ground-breaking play – *Look Back in Anger* or *The Birthday Party* for example – first made its impact on the stage. The gain is that historical perspective enables the critic to see more clearly what is significant and what is not, and to set each play in a broader context.

Two themes stand out as one examines 20th-century British drama. The first is that the century witnessed the growing sense that the theatre was not an aristocratic pleasure ground, but a democratic theatre for all. The long-awaited opening of the National Theatre in 1976 was an expression of this sense of theatre's importance for the whole community. The second theme is that of the role of women. From the beginning of the century in the works of G.B. Shaw to the end of the century with its 'post-feminist' theatre, this theme has absorbed dramatists.

In a book about drama, the question of audience or reader is an important one. In a way drama is to do with 'texts' just as any other form of literature. The written word may be examined by all the critical tools that are available. However, the reader must always be aware that the finished form of drama is not a reading but a performance. To that end, not only the text of *Twentieth Century British Drama* but also the tasks and assignments often point to a sense of the play in performance in the theatre.

The aim of the book is to give the reader the confidence to make his or her own informed judgements about British drama, and throughout the book there are various tasks and assignments designed to stimulate a personal response and to lead towards further exploration. Through engaging with these tasks, the student may experience some of the excitement of British drama in the 20th century.

For the purposes of this book 'British' is defined as relating to England, Scotland, Wales and Northern Ireland. This excludes modern Eire. As Shaw lived in England for nearly all his life and as all works first appeared on the London stage, it would seem pedantic to exclude such an important figure.

The dates given for plays are those of the first British performance.

How this book is organised

Part 1: Approaching 20th-century British drama
The aim of this part is to give an historical, social and cultural introduction to British drama and to outline the work of the major dramatic movements and dramatists.

Part 2: Approaching the texts
This part focuses on the artistic and dramatic qualities of the texts and how to interpret them.

Part 3: Play extracts
Part 3 is a selection of extracts, some central and well-known and some relatively inaccessible. All these extracts relate to the issues discussed in the book or form a focus for discussion in tasks and assignments.

Part 4: Critical approaches to 20th-century British drama
This part contains both general criticism and a selection of critics discussing one play in detail.

Part 5: How to write about 20th-century British drama
Part 5 aims to offer guidance to students about how to approach written tasks on 20th-century British drama, using a wide selection of assignments to focus on the issues raised by the book.

Part 6: Resources
This part contains:

- guidance on further reading, including critical works and books that enable the reader to explore the background to the texts
- a glossary defining the main critical terms used in the book. Critical terms that appear in bold type may be checked in the glossary
- a chronology relating texts to their contexts
- an index.

At different points throughout the book, and at the end of Parts 1, 2, 4 and 5 there are tasks and assignments designed to encourage the reader to reflect upon the material.

1 | Approaching 20th-century British drama

- How does 20th-century British drama relate to its social, cultural and historical context?

- What are the major theatrical movements and genres of the 20th century?

- How have individual playwrights developed and shaped their distinctive dramatic forms?

The Edwardian age

A conventional image of the years before the First World War is that of the 'long Edwardian summer', with ladies in elegant hats and dresses parading on the lawns of country houses. It is an England that belongs to the upper classes; an England of unruffled pace, secure in its sense of the rightfulness and permanence of its privileges. This image, popularised with romantic hindsight after the horrors of the war, concealed the reality of the situation.

When Queen Victoria died in 1901, Britain ruled the largest empire the world had ever seen. A quarter of the world's population was under British rule and the British navy ruled the seas. The Industrial Revolution had put Britain ahead of its European rivals and allowed it to become the largest trading nation and banker to the world. It seemed to some that this golden summer could never end.

Social conflicts

However, there were underlying problems. Having led the world in many of the great inventions of the 19th century, Britain fell behind in the newer industries of the 20th. Industrial competitors had caught up fast, and many eyes turned to Germany with an admiration that quickly changed to fear.

In a society in which it was said that 1% of the population owned 70% of the wealth, the rigidity of the class system and its inequalities came under scrutiny from a Liberal government led by Asquith (1908–1914), from the growing number of socialists and from the unemployed. Many of the tensions of the time were focused on industry. In an increasingly competitive market, the relationship of the workers to employers came under strain. This was the context in which the Labour Party was born in 1900. Legislation was passed that made strike action near to impossible and, as a result of the ensuing outcry, was just as quickly repealed. Industrial relations deteriorated when prices went up, but wages stayed the same.

Between 1910 and 1912 there were strikes by dockers, miners and railwaymen. The organised and strengthened unions were now clearly a powerful force, and, when a Triple Alliance of the three largest unions was formed in 1914, it seemed that confrontation was inevitable. Rarely can a play have caught the spirit of the moment as accurately as John Galsworthy's *Strife* (1909) which centres on a strike in Trenartha Tin Plate works and the conflict between the starving miners and the Board of Directors.

It was not only conflict in industry that seemed to be reaching a crisis point: in Ireland, Nationalists were beginning to plan rebellion and Unionists were preparing for armed resistance; in England, the suffragette movement transformed a political protest into a campaign of violent action. No wonder then that the newly established **repertory theatre** and its advanced thinkers were full of ideas and questions about the ills of society and of capitalism. George Bernard Shaw's socialist ideas were shared by Granville Barker who exposed the corruption of the family business in *The Voysey Inheritance* (1905), and the whole world of the couture industry from retail drapery to high fashion in *The Madras House* (1910). The repertory theatre brought society's problems to the audience's attention and gave voice to the underclass.

'The woman question'

Women were arguably the largest underclass in the Edwardian era. Emmeline Pankhurst founded the Women's Social and Political Union in 1903. Under her influence what had begun as a campaign of direct action became more and more a campaign of violence. Theatrical in their protests, sometimes even wearing the arrowhead costume of convicts, the suffragettes used the resources of drama to the full. Sketches and playlets were performed in halls and schools throughout the country and provided a forerunner to the **agit-prop** theatre of the 1930s. The Actresses' Franchise League was formed and Elizabeth Robins' *Votes for Women* (1907) whose centrepiece is the realistic re-enactment of a suffragette rally in Trafalgar Square, was enthusiastically performed throughout the country. The violent death of Emily Davison, fatally injured under the feet of the king's racehorse in the 1913 Derby, drew dramatic attention to the issue, but the active role of women working as nurses and ambulance drivers in the First World War probably did more to change perceptions. The granting of votes to women in 1918 was a natural extension of their war effort, but even then they had to wait another ten years before achieving the vote on equal terms with men. The developing sense of women's rights and of their roles in society is a major theme of the 20th century and its drama.

▶ Think of a play that you have seen either in the theatre or on television that has made you think about a particular issue, and perhaps made you reconsider your own position on it. How did it make its points and try to convince you?

▶ What are the advantages and disadvantages of using drama to promote a cause?

The Edwardian theatre

Theatre in Edwardian times was essentially London-based and provided a sense of occasion for those who could afford it. Theatres offered the upper and middle classes an opportunity to see and be seen in splendid surroundings. Ladies and gentlemen, dressed formally in evening dress, sat in ornately decorated comfort in one of the grand theatres of the West End of London. They might see a Shakespearean comedy in which a naturalistic set of dazzling beauty earned a round of applause as the curtains opened; or the 'Never-Never Land' of J.M. Barrie's *Peter Pan* (1904). There might be some thought-provoking moments, but the keynotes were entertainment and spectacle.

The actor-manager

At the centre of the performance was the star himself – perhaps the famous Henry Irving at the Lyceum, or Herbert Beerbohm Tree riding a snow-white horse at His Majesty's. These were the great actor-managers of their day and the central figures of the theatrical system. Like the great magnates of industry, they controlled all aspects of their world. They paid the wages, rehearsed the cast, were responsible for the theatre itself – and, of course, took the leading roles in the plays they directed. Many consequences flowed from this structure. To maximise profits and to make full use of an elaborate set, a long run was eminently desirable. Plays that made too many demands on the audience or touched on difficult or uncomfortable subjects were unsuitable.

M'COMAS	… There is only one place in all England where your opinions would still pass as advanced.
MRS CLANDON	[scornfully unconvinced] The Church, perhaps?
M'COMAS	No: the theatre …

This extract from Bernard Shaw's play *You Never Can Tell* (1897) sums up the conservatism of the commercial theatre of Edwardian times. The theatre of H.A. Jones (1851–1929) and Arthur Wing Pinero (1855–1934) was not without ideas and sharpness, but it was confined within its social and artistic straitjacket. The judgement of a contemporary Italian visitor was that 'The entire organisation of the theatre reflects that special and aristocratic conception of its status which is the point of view of its patrons.'

▶ Look carefully at the listings for the London West End theatre published in any broadsheet newspaper. Try to find out what kinds of play they are, then put them into columns under the heading of their types. Suggested columns might be: classic drama; Shakespeare; modern drama; musicals.

What conclusions can you draw about today's commercial theatre? How might the Edwardian theatre have differed?

The music hall

If the upper and middle classes enjoyed the West End, the working classes had a theatre of their own in the music hall, but its appeal was to so general an audience that it has been called the national theatre of its day. Music halls flourished in London and throughout the country. Their stars became national legends – Marie Lloyd, Dan Leno and Vesta Tilley – and their comedy, romance and slapstick fed straight into the silent films of Laurel and Hardy, and Charlie Chaplin. What the music hall offered was a closer reflection of the lives led by its audience, softened by romance and brightened by humour. Its pervasive influence was to be seen later in the 20th century in the work of television comedians such as Morecambe and Wise, whose training was in music hall; in the two desperate clowns of Samuel Beckett's *Waiting for Godot* (1955); in the music hall format of *Oh, What a Lovely War!* (1963), and even in the 'stand-up' comedy of today.

The new theatre: the influence of Ibsen and Shaw

There was another kind of theatre developing whose relative lack of popularity at the time belied its significance. The Norwegian playwright Henrik Ibsen's play, *Ghosts*, came to London in 1888, and scandalised critics and public alike.

The theme of the play - syphilis – struck at the heart of the revered institution of the family, and the brooding seriousness of the tone was at the opposite extreme to the 'entertainment' that conventional theatregoers expected. *A Doll's House* (1879) put the central dilemmas of women's freedom in a stifling and corrupt bourgeois setting. Ibsen's plays represented the beginnings of modern European drama. His influence in establishing a serious drama based on moral and social issues hung over what has been called 'the minority theatre', represented by the playwrights who did not write for the audiences of popular West End theatres, but for the smaller playhouses, repertory theatres and clubs which were beginning to establish themselves in London and the provinces.

Ibsen's champion in England was George Bernard Shaw, and it was through his plays that Ibsen's influence on the British stage was most clearly felt. It is hard to overstate Shaw's influence as writer, reviewer, critic and producer. His biting wit and experience as a man of the theatre helped him to make the minority theatre a commercial and popular success.

The new drama demanded a new, simpler staging and a new kind of theatre. The Court Theatre, under the directorship of Harley Granville Barker (1877–1946) from 1904–1907, became the leading avant-garde theatre in London. (As the Royal Court, 50 years later in 1956, this theatre was to assume the same role with its production of John Osborne's *Look Back in Anger*.) Shaw, whose plays formed the basis of the programme, wrote with characteristic immodesty that the first Court season marked 'the most important event in the history of the British stage since Shakespeare and Burbage ran the Globe Theatre on Bankside'.

Certainly the Court established some of the approaches which were to influence theatre in the 20th century. The convention of the long run was replaced by a repertory system. This allowed a much more daring approach, as a play that failed could be deleted from the repertoire without major difficulty or financial loss. The role of the actor-manager was replaced by the novel idea of the director who had overall control of the production. This development was pushed to its logical conclusion in the work of Gordon Craig (1872–1966). The idea of the central role of the director is one that is almost taken for granted in today's theatre.

The importance of Shaw

Shaw's theatrical career and influence spanned the centuries. In the late 1890s and the first years of the 20th century, he wrote a series of comedies that were to challenge, amuse and shock his audiences. From the social dramas of the 1890s, *Widowers' Houses* (1892) and *Mrs Warren's Profession* (published 1898 and first performed 1902), to the Edwardian plays such as *Major Barbara* (1905) and *Pygmalion* (1914), to post-war masterpieces such as *Saint Joan* (1924), Shaw's output was as prolific as it was varied. His account of Ibsen's dramatic strategy is as much an account of his own: 'Ibsen substituted a terrible art of sharp-shooting at the audience, trapping them, fencing with them, aiming always at the sorest spot in their consciences.' It was partly for this reason that Shaw called his first collection *Plays Unpleasant* (1898). Their subject matter, too, was 'unpleasant' – prostitution, profiteering and philandering.

Shaw was a man of ideas and his view of the theatre was that it had a serious purpose: to make people think. If that sounds commonplace today, it was much less so in Edwardian Britain. But, if the serious were the only side to Shaw, his work would be little performed and quickly forgotten. Shaw was also an entertainer, who invented a cast of comic characters as varied as those of Dickens. The German playwright, Bertolt Brecht, saw clearly the distinctive quality of Shaw's drama when he wrote in 1926:

It will have been observed that Shaw is a terrorist. Shaw's brand of terror is an extraordinary one, and he uses an extraordinary weapon, that of humour … Shaw's terrorism consists in this: that he claims a right for every man to act in all circumstances with decency, logic and humour.

(Brecht on Theatre, 1964)

In other words, Shaw's wit is not decorative, but essential to his purpose.

Unlike Brecht, Shaw had no radical or original approach to staging or to plot. He used the familiar forms of romance, historical chronicle and melodrama. What he did achieve, however, was to give each of the familiar plots his own twist, to surprise an audience and to frustrate their expectations. Surprises and reversals are embedded in Shaw's plots, and in the verbal wit for which his plays are known.

Pygmalion

Pygmalion (1914) is the story of a flower girl metamorphosed into a society lady by Professor Higgins, who teaches her phonetics so effectively that she is mistaken for a duchess. Shaw's point about the superficiality of class distinctions is well made, but Eliza's change from mechanical speaking doll to a live woman who is on equal terms with her creator leads an audience to expect the 'fairy tale' ending of the princess marrying the crusty bachelor and reforming him by showing him a humanity he lacked. From the time the first actor played Higgins and threw red roses at Eliza between the end of the play and the final curtain, to the film adaptation in *My Fair Lady*, Shaw's ending has been altered or seen as unsatisfactory. Shaw deliberately set up and then rejected the romantic ending as sentimental. By denying the conventional ending, Shaw left Eliza's future open and made the audience revise its expectations.

Shaw's plays of ideas

Just as his endings teased and surprised, so Shaw constantly challenged expectations of character. **Melodrama**, **farce** and the **well-made play** all tend to rely on the hero and villain. The audience's moral bearings are made clear in a simplified world. Shaw would have none of this and repudiated the idea of the villain, using the touchstone of what is true to life – a standard that he invoked against all forms of falsity and the artificial:

The average man is covetous, lazy, selfish; but he is not malevolent, nor capable of saying to himself, 'Evil: be thou my good'. He only does wrong as a means to an end, which he always represents to himself as a right end. The case is exactly reversed with a villain …

(quoted in Eric Bentley Bernard Shaw, 1975)

Just as the villain may be a dramatic fiction, so may the hero: in fact heroism, like idealism, was always likely to be debunked in Shaw's drama. Apparent villains like Mrs Warren, in *Mrs Warren's Profession* (1902), who organises prostitutes, or Andrew Undershaft, the capitalist arms manufacturer in *Major Barbara* (1905), are allowed to make their cases forcefully. Undershaft himself is seen as a model employer and a hater of the true evil of poverty. Indeed, as Shaw wrote in discussing the plays of Ibsen (*Major Critical Essays*, 1986), this moral uncertainty was exactly what distinguished the new drama:

> In the new plays, the drama arises through a conflict of unsettled ideals … [and] is not between clear right and wrong … the question that makes the play interesting is which is the villain and which the hero.

In place of the traditional resolution of a knotty plot, Shaw wrote discussions, refining and clarifying the issues. Discussion is thus of key importance in Shaw's drama. All his heroes and heroines are, in a sense, polished debaters, but the wit they show is not the epigrammatic wit of Oscar Wilde, but rather the best expression of their convictions.

Shaw's early plays revealed the hypocrisies of society, and his later ones drew attention to its complexities and dilemmas. His alteration of the traditional **genres**, and the simplified characterisation which these genres implied, was ultimately a rejection of the simplified and false view of the world they represented. His achievement was that he opened up the stage for serious debate and proved that it could be invigorating. It was not until the 1960s that the challenge of Shaw's political and moral theatre was taken up once more.

▶ How important are ideas in the theatre? What is the difference between a dramatised debate and a play of ideas? Read the extract from *Our Country's Good* (Part 3, pages 92–94). Note down your impressions of how Timberlake Wertenbaker contrasts the characters and their views. Look closely at the language of each character and the way characters interact. Which is the key speech in this extract? Does the dramatist successfully convey her main arguments to you?

The growth of the new theatre

The repertory movement became unstoppable and was closely linked with regional and provincial theatre. Most notable was the founding of the Abbey Theatre in Dublin, but throughout the country, repertory theatres were established as fast as Theatre Royals had been in Victorian times. The repertory movement came to Glasgow in 1909 and Liverpool in 1910; in 1913 the Birmingham Repertory

Theatre opened. This was the first theatre specifically built for a repertory company.

Perhaps the most influential of the companies was that founded at the Gaiety Theatre, Manchester, by Miss Horniman in 1908. Here a strong local tradition found its voice in the plays of the industrial north of Allan Monkhouse, Stanley Houghton and Harold Brighouse – the so-called Manchester School – which represented working class life with a sympathy and a humour born of close observation. Clayton Holmes, an American critic, wrote in 1917 that the 'two greatest theatres in the British Isles are the Abbey Theatre in Dublin and the Gaiety in Manchester'.

Arthur Wing Pinero outlined the future of the theatre under the influence of Ibsen. He looked forward to 'a drama based wholly on observation and experience, which lays aside the worn-out puppets and proverbs of the theatre and illustrates faithfully modern social life'. However, he was not the playwright who expressed these aims in the theatre: it was left to Shaw, Harley Granville Barker and John Galsworthy (1867–1933) in London, the Abbey Theatre in Dublin and the Manchester School to develop a drama to meet the challenge of the times.

▶ Find out as much as you can about your local theatre. When was it built? How has it changed? Can you define the kind of audience it attracts? What sort of plays does it put on? How has its role in the community changed since it was built?

A theatre of ideas and of social comment risked dryness and dullness. It was to the credit of many of the Edwardian dramatists that their characters lived on stage to such an extent that the audience did not feel they had been buttonholed to listen to a dramatic lecture or sermon. Or perhaps the intensity of the issues and conflicts that the drama embodied carried its own charge of dramatic energy.

The drama very often centred on a family and explored the conflicts between the younger generation and the older. The older generation was typically represented by an unyielding patriarchal figure whose values, but not necessarily conduct, were Victorian. The struggle between the generations often involved the rights and freedoms of a young woman who found herself in conflict because she did not want to marry her lover (Stanley Houghton's *Hindle Wakes*, 1912); wanted to divorce (Granville Barker's *The Voysey Inheritance*); or to have an abortion (*Waste*, 1906–1907). The plays were set firmly in the world of work and of business: Galsworthy's *Strife* starts six months into a strike by workers in the Trenartha Tin Plate Works; *The Voysey Inheritance* is based on a lawyer's practice, and even the lighter comedy of *Hobson's Choice* (1915) by Harold Brighouse is an entirely believable picture of work in a northern cobbler's. These firmly established settings allowed the dramatists to give force to their analyses of class and the financial bases of power relationships.

What happened in the theatre in the early years of this century was an outburst of dramatic energy. In many ways the Edwardian stage acted as a prologue to the themes of the century: the division between the commercial theatre and the smaller, poorer, but ultimately much more important theatre that we associate with the repertory movement and the 'little theatres'; the sense of theatre mediating to a wider audience the crucial issues of the moment, rather than being an exclusive entertainment for the upper and middle classes; the movement away from London's West End to the provinces; the presentation of working class people on stage. All these would find echoes and restatements throughout the century.

▶ What do you think were the two or three main issues that were most important to Edwardian playwrights? What are the three major issues that seem most important to dramatists today? Note down the main similarities and differences.

▶ Read carefully the extracts from *Hindle Wakes* and *Hobson's Choice* (Part 3, pages 72–76). How far and in what ways do they reflect the social and political issues discussed above?

The Great War and after

The Great War, as those who lived through the First World War called it, killed more than half a million British soldiers. Enormously popular to begin with, the 'war to end all wars' was expected to be over by Christmas 1914. Young men hurried to join up and Britain, unlike other combatant nations, did not need to introduce conscription until 1916. The experience of the war, which was the first war to be fought using tanks, aeroplanes and the technology of mass destruction, was to mark a generation of young men and their families. The picture we have today is coloured by the art, poetry and prose that came from the soldiers in the trenches. Siegfried Sassoon's accounts of the life of an infantry officer, Wilfred Owen's immediately powerful poetry, and Paul Nash's pictures of a barren and shell-blasted landscape are just a few examples from a war which produced so many artistic witnesses and commentators – but surprisingly little drama.

The state of the nation

Immediately after the Armistice in 1918, Lloyd George, the Prime Minister in the last years of the war, called an election to gain the peace vote and was re-elected. His post-war programme was one of reconstruction with an emphasis on increased welfare provision. He famously promised 'a land fit for heroes' to the returning soldiers, but to many it seemed that little had changed despite all the wartime sacrifices. The economic and social problems that were to blight the inter-war years soon became apparent. The cotton mills of Manchester, the dockyards of the Clyde, the Tyne and the Wear, and the mining industry of South Wales, were some of the areas where the promises of Lloyd George must have sounded exceptionally hollow. It was in exactly these regions that workers' theatre grew.

The General Strike of 1926

When worsening economic conditions led the coal owners to demand a reduction in miners' wages, the miners went on strike. They were supported by the Trades Union Congress and the Labour Party. Nearly four million strikers came out in support of the miners. When middle class university students drove trams and buses in defiance of the strike and 5000 strikers were arrested, the country was divided. The General Strike was all over in nine days once the TUC decided to end their support, and all but the miners gave in. The resulting divisions in society were deep rooted. These divisions were expressed in the play *In Time o' Strife* by a Scottish miner, Joe Corrie, that premiered in Glasgow in 1927.

'The Gay Twenties'

Against this background of hardship there was another side to the 1920s. In America, Scott Fitzgerald named it the Jazz Age and, in England, the *Daily Mail* coined the phrase 'the bright Young Things'. Both referred to that post-war phenomenon of the young casting aside their parents' values and living their lives in new and daring ways. It would be wrong to exaggerate a social change that affected the rich more than the poor, but the publicity that the new fashions, music and styles attracted made sure that all were aware of this glittering new world of style and money.

'The Twenties were at least as gay as the Thirties would be over cast' wrote the theatre critic and historian J.C. Trewin. 'Few thought seriously of another war; the world in recovery was expanding ... naturally the theatre reflected this age of relaxed conventions, of fervid good cheer and questing experiment.' Trewin concluded that it was a decade which could be best summed up in a popular tune of the time:

> On New Year's Eve, 1929 ... a sour wind sighed round the once heedless theatre of amusement, but the song that beat up against the tears still had the rhythm of the Gay Twenties:
> I want to be happy,
> But I won't be happy
> Till I've made *you* happy too.

Noel Coward

Noel Coward depicted and embodied the moneyed and escapist world of the 1920s and 1930s. *The Sketch* of 29 April 1925 wrote of him as 'probably the most famous man of his age in England as he is but twenty-five and is the author of two plays running in town – *The Vortex* and *Fallen Angels*'. Coward played the lead in *The Vortex* (1924), a 'much praised and constantly discussed drama'. Coward himself said that the play 'established me both as a playwright and as an actor' and allowed him 'the trappings of success,' which included a car, 'silk shirts and an extravagant amount of pyjamas and dressing gowns'.

The Vortex and *Hay Fever*

At the centre of *The Vortex* is the relationship between Florence Lancaster, a brilliantly dressed young-looking mother, and her 24-year-old son, Nicky, who has just returned from Paris to tell his mother of his recent engagement. His mother, however, is preoccupied with her lover, Tom Veryan, who is the same age as Nicky but contrasts with him in every other way.

In the final act, Nicky confronts his mother in an attempt to make her face the truth of her age and the responsibilities she has to her husband and son. His drug taking (a very controversial and shocking topic at the time) and her serial adultery are at least partly caused by a sick society. He tells his mother that 'it's not your fault – it's the fault of circumstances and civilisation – civilisation makes rottenness so much easier – we're utterly rotten – both of us – we swirl about in a vortex of beastliness'. As the tears roll down her face, Florence strokes her son's hair 'mechanically in an effort to calm him' and the curtain falls. Coward's plays rarely offer tidy resolutions.

Had Coward's career ended with *The Vortex*, he might have been seen as a satiric moralist. The play gives a bitter account of the social world of sexual desire and artistic pretension. No wonder that Coward could defend his play against the censor as 'little more than a moral tract'.

After the success of *The Vortex*, Coward's next play to be produced was *Hay Fever* (1925), a play whose frivolity, geniality and pace of action made it an immediate hit – Coward said: 'It is considered by many to be my best comedy'. Although very different in tone and characterisation from *The Vortex*, it nonetheless continued the theme of shifting partnerships.

Cavalcade

Perhaps Coward's outstanding success, and a play that seemed to catch the mood of the nation, was *Cavalcade* (1930–1931). With its theme of the pageant of English history, Coward had produced a play of epic proportions. The play's 22 scenes begin with the Boer War and follow the events of the early 20th century through the eyes of a middle class family and its servants. Domestic scenes alternate with public ones as the impact of the century is measured in the suffering and the pride of the family. Coward packed the stage with 400 extras to make the crowd scenes as spectacular as he possibly could. The final stage directions indicated the blend of effects Coward was looking for:

> Noise grows louder and louder. Steam rivets, loudspeakers, jazz bands, aeroplane propellers, etc., until the general effect is complete chaos.
> Suddenly it all fades into darkness and silence and away at the back a Union Jack glows through the blackness.

When King George V and Queen Mary came to see the play, cast and audience joined in singing 'God Save the King' amid scenes of patriotic fervour. Coward's reputation was at its peak.

The play is central because it was seen at the time as 'the play of the century', and because its presentation of history strangely foreshadowed not only Joan Littlewood's *Oh, What a Lovely War!* but also the 'state of the nation' plays of the 1980s, though from a very different political perspective. In developing a wit that comes from character and situation, Coward paved the way for Joe Orton, and in developing the plots of tangled sexual relationships and their complicated geometry, he can be compared to Alan Ayckbourn.

Coward was a major playwright of the 1920s and early 1930s. Despite his limitations, he held up a mirror to his times reflecting the wit and gaiety of his generation and class. His plays present a glamorous wasteland with a mixture of fascination and loathing.

The 1930s

The Wall Street Crash of 1929 not only ruined the lives of thousands of Americans, it also affected the financial markets throughout the world. The economic depression which followed and the rise in unemployment in Britain to two and a half million in 1931 set the keynote for the whole decade. The spectre of poverty and hardship became a reality as the hunger marchers from Jarrow in the north east marched on the capital in 1936. At a time when capitalism seemed hard to defend morally, it also seemed to many to have failed to deliver prosperity and jobs. Many thinkers saw in the economic crises of the 1930s the fulfilment of Marx's ideas that capitalism was doomed. They began to look with admiration at Russian communism, which seemed to offer a fairer and a more efficient system.

The crisis was not only a domestic one. Germany was turning towards fascism:

economic crisis and the rise of Adolf Hitler pointed to threatening times ahead. Politics in Britain were becoming more extreme as fascists fought communists in the East End of London. The Spanish Civil War crystallised the struggle between the forces of socialism and those of fascism, and many young British men rushed to Spain to fight for the left as socialists or anarchists.

Workers' theatre

The commercial theatre of London's West End remained insulated from the pressures and economic realities of the time, offering little for the politically aware. A more direct response came from the workers' political groups that established themselves throughout Britain in the 1930s. This was theatre at the opposite extreme to the West End. Many working class left wing groups formed themselves into companies of actors to inform, educate and propagandise. They called on the working class to understand the issues, and went onto the streets or to the factory gates to put over their message. The names of the companies tell us a good deal about their purpose: 'Theatre of Action', 'Red Megaphones', 'Unity.'

The rulebook of Unity, London, defined its purpose: 'To foster the art of drama by interpreting life as it is experienced by the majority of the people, to work for the betterment of society.' Theatre groups like Unity took their plays to where people worked, acting out scenes at the factory gates, on the street corners, in canteens and clubs. They swept away many of the trappings associated with British theatre – high prices, evening dress and a middle class audience watching its own reflection on the stage. The conventional **Fourth wall naturalism** was obviously unsuited to this kind of theatre and the groups developed new ways of getting their message across. Pantomime and broad humour were often used, as was choral declamation and socialist **realism**. Agit-prop (a contraction of 'agitational propaganda') was derived from Soviet Russia. The **Living Newspaper** style, borrowed from the American Federal Theatre, allowed an immediate topicality of reference. The Unity, London, presented, for example, the Munich Crisis as a Living Newspaper. The Prime Minister, Chamberlain, became a wicked Uncle in *Babes in the Wood* and political satire in drama was born.

From the 1930s until just after the Second World War, the workers' theatre movement presented a commentary on events and voiced a left wing – sometimes a communist – response to them. It had a truly European perspective and staged the first productions of Brecht and Jean-Paul Sartre in Britain. Its importance lay not so much in the plays that emerged – although there were many of merit like Joe Corrie's *In Time o' Strife* – but in the ways in which it broadened the sense of what theatre was for and how it could be performed. Joan Littlewood's roots lay in the movement and the upsurge of British theatre in the 1960s was built on these earlier foundations.

▶ Read the extract from *Their Theatre and Ours* (Part 3, pages 76–78) and discuss the ways in which Tom Thomas outlines the difference between the two kinds of theatre.

The commercial theatre

It must not be forgotten, however, that especially for the middle class, the inter-war period was one of increasing material prosperity and comfort. House building went on apace, wages rose and for many this was an era of new found leisure. Sport flourished and this was the golden age of crossword puzzles, contract bridge and detective fiction. Real poverty remained in many of the regions, but for most of southern Britain it was a time of growing prosperity.

The commercial theatre catered for the predominantly middle class audience with a largely escapist diet. Ivor Novello wrote a series of enormously successful musical revues for Drury Lane, including *Glamorous Night* (1935), *Careless Rapture* (1936) and *The Dancing Years* (1939). Dancing girls were always popular, as were fantasies set in exotic locations. The two most commercially successful playwrights were Noel Coward and Ben Travers. As composer, song-writer and dramatist, Coward dominated the West End stage from *Hay Fever* in 1925 to *Blithe Spirit* in 1941. Travers wrote a series of ten farces that occupied the stage of the Aldwych continuously from 1925 to 1933, and he and his two leading actors, Tom Walls and Ralph Lynn 'set the tone of English comedy between the wars'. The popularity of the theatre, however, faced a new challenge from the cinema.

The cinema and the advent of radio

This post-war generation with its new-found money sought its entertainment in the cinema, which enjoyed a golden age of popularity in the 1930s. With the weight and glamour of Hollywood behind it and the advent of the 'talkies', the cinema became powerful enough to threaten the theatre. Many theatres were converted to cinemas. Stars such as Laurel and Hardy, Rudolph Valentino and Lillian Gish became household names. In 1939, 20 million cinema tickets were sold each week, and cinema was able to reach out to a widespread and genuinely mixed audience. At home, the radio offered a new awareness of events and provided affordable entertainment. Small wonder that the provincial theatre nearly died and London's West End struggled.

W.H. Auden and the Group Theatre

Apart from workers' theatre groups, the other theatrical opposition to the West End came from the Group Theatre of W.H. Auden and Christopher Isherwood. Here experimental theatre was used to effect a radical agenda. Dance, poetry and choric

Choose therefore that you may recover: both your charity and
   your place
Determining not this that we have lately witnessed: but
   another country
Where grace may grow outward and be given praise
Beauty and virtue be vivid there.

Auden's dream of a new kind of poetic theatre that was both popular and serious did not come about, but his experimental approach created a sense of the possible and mapped the ground for others to explore.

T.S. Eliot and verse drama

T.S. Eliot and Auden shared many ideas about drama. Both rejected naturalism. Both, however, believed that it was imperative to use the popular forms of the time. Both believed that the judgement of an audience was crucial and, above all, both came to the theatre as poets and felt that the language of the theatre needed the blood transfusion of poetry.

Eliot's dramatic verse developed from his first fragmentary play, *Sweeney Agonistes* (1928), in which he used the popular rhythms of jazz and the musical to create a mood that is sinister, comic and unexpected. In *Murder in the Cathedral* (1935), a play written for a specifically Christian audience in a cathedral, Eliot allowed himself full use of rich poetic imagery. In his later plays, however, Eliot moved towards a much sparer style. Thus, he designed a verse that was as unobtrusive as it was plain. Some critics believed that he compromised too much with the requirements of naturalistic drama and that his verse became insipid at this stage; others felt that the very austerity gave it power.

Eliot's career as a dramatist was one of exploration. As a Christian, he needed to forge a verse drama that would express not the trivialities of the everyday, but the universal patterns beneath human experience. As he wrote in the essay 'Poetry and Drama':

It seems to me that beyond the nameable, classifiable emotions and motives of our conscious life when directed towards action – the part of life which prose drama is wholly adequate to express – there is a fringe of indefinite extent, of feeling which we can only detect, so to speak, out of the corner of the eye and can never completely focus. There are great prose dramatists – such as Ibsen and Chekhov – who have done things of which I would not otherwise have supposed prose to be capable, but who seem to me, in spite of their success, to have been hampered by their writing in prose. This peculiar range of sensibility can be expressed by dramatic poetry, at its moments of greatest intensity. At such moments we touch the border of those feelings which only music can express.

The expression of these moments lay at the heart of Eliot's theory and practice.

Overview of the 1930s

During the 1930s Shaw continued to write comedies that challenged an audience to think about its own comfortable assumptions and to question society's values. In Noel Coward's plays there was much more than mere frothy entertainment. In the workers' theatre groups there were the beginnings of a political sense of theatre, and what theatre is for. In the theatre of Auden there was a genuinely radical mixture of styles that ranged from pantomime to high seriousness. T.S. Eliot tested his theories about verse drama in a series of remarkable plays, of which *Murder in the Cathedral* is the best known.

Radio drama was in its infancy, but its 'blindness' made it suitable for all kinds of poetic effect which led to later masterpieces such as Louis Macneice's *Dark Tower* (1946) and Dylan Thomas' *Under Milk Wood* (1953).

After the Second World War

The Second World War ended in 1945 and, to enormous surprise, Labour defeated Winston Churchill and the Conservatives in the General Election of that year. The new Labour government, whose manifesto was called 'Let's Face the Future,' set about the creation of the Welfare State. The National Health Service was introduced and free medical treatment became generally available. There was free secondary education for all after the Education Act of 1944, and the expansion and construction of new universities: Jimmy Porter in *Look Back in Anger* was one of the first products of a university that was 'white tile', not redbrick. National Insurance legislation was broadened to include all workers, and National Assistance was introduced. Retirement pensions became available to all. J.B. Priestley's *An Inspector Calls* (1946) expressed this sense of responsibility of the individual to the wider society in the Inspector's warning to the Birling family:

> But just remember this. One Eva Smith has gone – but there are millions and millions and millions of Eva Smiths and John Smiths still left with us, with their lives, their hopes and fears, their suffering and their chance of happiness, all intertwined with our lives, and what we think and say and do. We don't live alone. We are members of one body. We are responsible for each other. And I tell you that the time will soon come when, if men will not learn that lesson, then they will be taught it in fire and blood and anguish.

Terence Rattigan and post-war theatre

The immediate post-war period was one of reconstruction in which nearly everyone could find a job, slums were cleared, higher wages allowed the prospect of travel abroad and new universities were founded. However in the theatre, just as in the period after the First World War, there was little sense of the changing times.

The leading figure of the time was Terence Rattigan whose well-made plays often contained a much less conventional **sub-text**. His plays, like those of his mentor Noel Coward, dealt with homosexuality obliquely or by implication, as before 1968 there was an absolute ban on homosexuality as a dramatic theme. So Rattigan based his play *Ross* (1960) on the life of T.E. Lawrence and hinted that his 'abnormal' character was the result of Turkish torture and sexual abuse. The reticence of this treatment might be compared with a notoriously explicit scene of homosexual rape in Howard Brenton's *The Romans in Britain* (1980) to show how completely the sense of what was acceptable on stage changed in the space of 20 years. It is unsurprising, given Rattigan's homosexuality, that his plays should deal with characters who find the expression of emotion difficult, with the suppressed and the repressed individual. The central figure in *The Browning Version* (1948) is an ageing failure of a schoolmaster, 'the Himmler of the Lower Fifth'. When he is forced to take early retirement, a boy gives him a parting gift and he has to cover his feelings by turning his back to take some heart medicine. The critic Harold Hobson wrote of a production in which Eric Portman played the schoolmaster:

> The audience could not restrain its tears; and when his wife cruelly remarked that the gift was not a sign of affection or respect but merely a piece of astute policy to get a higher mark in an examination, a visible thrill ran through it. At that moment Portman hesitated whilst polishing his glasses. The action was barely perceptible, but Portman made it show how the whole pride of a man's life can be killed by one blow.
>
> (*Theatre in Britain*, 1984)

'Loamshire'

The young Kenneth Tynan hated the dominance of the well-made play and the drawing room comedy. He became theatre critic of the *Observer* in 1954 and used the fictional Home County of Loamshire in order to satirise the whole school of middle class drama that he hated so much:

> Its setting is a country house in what used to be called Loamshire but is now, as a heroic tribute to realism, sometimes called Berkshire. Except when someone must sneeze, or be murdered, the sun

inevitably shines. The inhabitants belong to a social class derived partly from romantic novels and partly from the playwright's vision of the leisured life he will lead after the play is a success … people of passionate intellectual appetites are losing heart, falling away, joining the queues outside the Curzon Cinema. To lure them home, the theatre must widen its scope, broaden its horizon so that Loamshire appears merely as the play-pen, not as the whole palace of drama. We need plays about cabmen and demi-gods, plays about warriors, politicians and grocers …

(Observer, 1954)

Subsequent criticism might take a kinder view of both Coward and Rattigan, stressing less the middle class and restricted nature of their vision, and more the sexual themes that dwell beneath the surface, as well as the craftsmanship of their plots. Nevertheless, the whole theatre of Coward, of Rattigan and of Priestley was finished off by the success of *Look Back in Anger* (1956) and the plays of working class life that followed it.

▶ Read the extract from *The Real Inspector Hound* (Part 3, pages 87–88) and discuss the conventions of characterisation, plot and setting that Stoppard is parodying. What plays or films that you know follow some of these conventions? How does Stoppard make them ridiculous?

Theatre after 1956: the birth of the 'angry young man'

1956 was a year of crisis. The Suez crisis arose when President Nasser of Egypt decided to nationalise the Suez Canal. Israel invaded Egypt, and Britain and France sent troops to the Canal Zone, allegedly to keep the peace between the Arabs and the Israelis. The war was short and ineffective, but what it demonstrated was more long-lasting. No longer could Britain consider itself a great power, free to relive its imperial past in military adventures throughout the world. Taking advantage of the world's distraction, Russian troops invaded Hungary to counter the threat of self-government. The television pictures of tanks crushing the revolt were so powerful that many British communists and left wingers lost all sympathy with the Soviet Union and communism. In Arnold Wesker's *Chicken Soup with Barley* (1958) the young Ronnie accosts his mother about her communism:

What has happened to all the comrades, Sarah? I even blush when I use that word. Comrade! Why do I blush? Why do I feel ashamed to use words like democracy and freedom and brotherhood? They don't have meaning any more. I have nothing to write about any more.

Look Back in Anger

The failure of the British government in the Suez Crisis and disillusion with communism led to a mood of frustration that is brilliantly evoked by John Osborne's *Look Back in Anger* (1956). It was a play that caught the moment with unerring accuracy, not primarily because of its dramatic qualities, but more because of its hero, Jimmy Porter. The expansion of university education helped to offer new opportunities for working class students. Jimmy Porter was the spokesman of these newly articulate young people:

> There aren't any good, brave causes left. If the big bang does come, and we all get killed off, it won't be in aid of the old-fashioned, grand design. It'll just be for the Brave New-nothing-very-much-thank-you. About as pointless and inglorious as stepping in front of a bus. No, there's nothing left for it, me boy, but to let yourself be butchered by the women.

It is worth quoting this famous speech in its context to show how broad the targets of the so-called 'angry young man' could be. There is nostalgia for an age of clear causes and commitment (Jimmy's father died of wounds received in the Spanish Civil War), there is a sense of life's futility in the shadow of the Bomb (CND, the Campaign for Nuclear Disarmament, was born just after *Look Back in Anger*), and there is an almost hysterical hatred of women. Perhaps this 'anger' can best be defined as a style and an approach: scornfully dismissive, harshly comic, but also sentimental and self-pitying. At any rate, Kenneth Tynan saw this as the kind of ground-breaking theatre

> ... one had despaired of ever seeing on the stage – the drift towards anarchy, the instinctive leftishness, the automatic rejection of 'official' attitudes, the surrealist sense of humour ... the casual promiscuity; the sense of lacking a crusade worth fighting for ...
>
> (*Observer*, 1956)

With these words, and with some help from the theatre publicity, the 'angry young man' was born. The label 'angry young man' became shorthand for a group of writers and their heroes who actually had little in common. For the theatre, *Look Back in Anger* meant the presentation of working class heroes and heroines, and the replacement of the middle class drawing room by the flat and the ironing board.

Three very different plays of 1958 developed the theatrical territory that Osborne had opened up. Shelagh Delaney's *A Taste of Honey* (1958) with its account of a pregnant teenager befriended by a homosexual; John Arden's *Live Like Pigs* (1958) set in a Northern housing estate, and Harold Pinter's *The Birthday*

Party (1958). The playwright and critic, Bernard Kops, noted the sea-change that had occurred in the theatre:

> The working classes have become articulate and young writers have sprung up all over the country, products of this special time, symptomatic of the great social changes that have taken place, perhaps the first bubbles of a mighty volcano.

There was clearly a group of young writers who felt a sense of common purpose as they stormed the establishment. Kops spoke for the whole group when he summarised their achievements:

> Theatre in England was no longer the precious inner sanctum for the precious few. Writers such as Shelagh Delaney, John Arden, Alun Owen, Robert Bolt, Willis Hall and myself have changed the face of things and we hope for all time. We write about the problems of the world today because we live in the world of today. We write about the young, because we are young. We write about Council flats and the H-bomb and racial discrimination because these things concern us and concern the young people of our country, so that if and when they come to the theatre, they will see that it is not divorced from reality, that it is for them, and they will feel at home.
>
> (*Jewish Chronicle*, 1956)

Drama in the age of television

Television became a feature of British life in 1953 when the broadcast of Queen Elizabeth's coronation captured millions of viewers. The growing popularity of television was remarkable, and by the end of the 1960s more than nine out of ten families owned a television set. How would the theatre accommodate itself to this newest and most popular of arts? Was it the greatest threat to live theatre since the 'talkies' or a grand opportunity to reach huge audiences?

At first, television drama was restricted to a static camera recording the stage performance. But television soon acquired a style of its own. With the advent of commercial television in 1954 came *Armchair Theatre*; in 1964 the BBC responded to the challenge with the *Wednesday Play*, renamed as *Play for Today* in 1970. Many writers of drama seized the opportunity to write for the new medium, and the drama that emerged was as challenging and socially aware as the theatre of the time. Jeremy Sandford's *Cathy Come Home* (1966) was but the best known of a whole series of plays. Its portrait of the plight of the homeless Cathy, trying to be reunited with her husband and children, was so effective in stirring opinion that it resulted in the founding of Shelter, the charity for the homeless. Trevor Griffiths, Alan Plater, Harold Pinter, Simon Gray and David Hare are just a few of those who wrote for both television and the stage. The work of Dennis Potter, from *Vote Vote Vote for Nigel Barton* (1965) to *The Singing Detective* (1986) and *Lipstick on Your Collar* (1993), developed an individual style using popular songs as a kind of Brechtian device to underline and comment on the material. It was masterly and innovative television.

Soaps and sitcoms

But it was not mainstream drama that provided the staple diet of television. From its start in 1960, *Coronation Street* held its viewers (of up to 29 million) for half an hour in two weekly episodes and made Elsie Tanner a household name. *Brookside*, based on a housing estate near Liverpool, and *EastEnders* looked more contemporary than their parent, but relied just as much on the interaction of a group of familiar and contrasting characters in a specific community. Soaps continue to hold huge audiences throughout the world.

Situation comedy shared some of the appeal of the soap. From *Hancock's Half-Hour* to *The Good Life* and *Yes, Minister*, the sitcom made its sharp and observant comments on everything from Railway Cuttings, Cheam to the corridors of power in Whitehall. *Men Behaving Badly* and *Harry Enfield and Friends* made telling points about their times too, and their appeal partly derived from the fact that many of their viewers were of the same age as the characters portrayed.

Despite the interplay between television and theatre, it is hard to measure the effect that television has had. The technology that records the 'real' and gives a close up of human reaction and feeling is at the opposite end of the spectrum to drama based on story telling and impersonation. There is, arguably, little point in an art that creates an illusion of the real when you have a camera. At the same time, theatre has tried to incorporate some of the techniques – and indeed technology – of television. The free-flowing changing of scene in Caryl Churchill's *Fen* (1983) or Patrick Marber's *Closer* (1997), for example, owe much to the fluidity and cross-cutting of television drama. Above all the television audience, unconditioned about what to expect from drama, allowed dramatists the freedom to experiment.

▶ What do you think are the main similarities and differences between television soaps and the drama that you are reading?

Beckett and Brecht

Two theatrical events were of enormous importance in the mid–1950s: *Waiting for Godot* by the Irish writer, Samuel Beckett, received its British premiere in 1955; and *Mother Courage* by the leading German playwright, Bertolt Brecht, was first staged in Britain in 1956.

No single play has had more influence on British drama this century than *Waiting for Godot*. It is the story of two tramps waiting for a man called Godot whom they don't know. The stage is entirely bare except for a tree and a mound. The dialogue is as pared down as the set and yet achieves a poetic truthfulness. This kind of writing was too original and strange for the reviewers and audience, and the first night was a disaster. Only Harold Hobson, the drama critic of *The Sunday Times*, was able to see the play's importance in a review he presciently entitled 'Tomorrow'.

It is through Beckett's work that **absurdist drama** reached Britain from Europe. In 1956, the Berliner Ensemble gave the British stage its first sight of **epic theatre**, with their production of Brecht's *Mother Courage*. This was a kind of theatre that was more political, more to do with 'reality' and less concerned with the emotional inner dramas that had for so long dominated the British stage. The production was as eye-opening as *Godot*, as it traced the fortunes of its stubbornly brave heroine across war-torn Europe. In the writing of Edward Bond, Howard Brenton, David Edgar and David Hare varieties of epic theatre were to become the mainstream drama of the 1970s and 1980s.

Brecht's influence on British theatre

Bertolt Brecht (1898–1956) has had a deep and wide-ranging influence on British theatre in the 20th century. Many of the ideas about what drama should be, and dramatic conventions that are now taken for granted come from his pioneering work as a director, dramatist and prolific critic. The fact that Brecht, himself a communist, was German and lived through the First World War and the rise of fascism in Hitler's Germany, ensured the passionate moral and political commitment of his theatre. His task was to devise a theatre which would be a lens on society and the agent of critical thought about it. His nationality and time made these tasks urgent and practical. How, as a practical man of the theatre, could he also attract and entertain his audience?

Brecht was so dissatisfied with the conventions of his day, because he felt that the clear purpose of theatre to combine entertainment and instruction could no longer be fulfilled. Hence, a new dramatic style had to evolve. In his essay on Experimental Theatre, Brecht asked:

> How can the theatre be both instructive and entertaining? How can it be divorced from spiritual dope traffic and turned from a home of illusions to a home of experience? How can the tortured and heroic, absurd and ingenious, changeable and world-changing man of this great and ghastly century obtain his own theatre, which will help him to master the world and himself?
>
> (*Brecht on Theatre*, 1964)

This was indeed a grand agenda and Brecht used the term 'epic theatre' to stress its social and heroic nature.

Brecht revolted against the convention of **naturalism** and the 'Fourth wall'. He did not want his actors to become their roles, but insisted on a critical distance between actor and role. The distance between the audience and the actor would echo that critical distance. The aim was to dispel the illusionist or magic sense of theatre and replace it with a critical, analytical response. This was Brecht's famous *Verfremdungseffekt* – literally a making strange – that has been called the Alienation Technique. From this, all kinds of consequences flowed. Rather like the kind of modern architecture that does not conceal all the functional parts of a building – the pipes and drains and cables – but uses them very visibly as part of the total architecture, Brecht ostentatiously drew attention to stage conventions, using songs, direct address to the audience, choric speech or summarising the contents of a scene on placards that were paraded on stage.

Characteristically there was a minimal set, very few props and stylised costumes that underlined the fact that the audience watched 'demonstrators' rather than actors. All of the theory and practice sprang from the central purpose – to make the audience think about their roles as citizens and the moral choices to be made. As Brecht saw it, the traditional theatre audience passively watching a play was the exact image of a people so absorbed in their roles in society that they failed to examine it critically. Passivity was the enemy in the theatre and on the street. So the theatre had to move out of the drawing room into the streets, and the focus was no longer on character but on society itself. Brecht's ideas of theatre underlay the work of Theatre Workshop and of playwrights like John Arden, Howard Barker and David Edgar who formed the mainstream in British theatre in the 1970s and early 1980s.

▶ Brecht proposed a basic model for his epic theatre. This was a street scene 'in which an eyewitness demonstrates to a crowd of onlookers how a road accident took place. The bystanders may or may not have seen what happened, or they may see things in a different way: the point is that the demonstrator acts the behaviour of driver or victim or both in such a way that the bystanders are able to form an opinion about the accident.'

Act this scene out and then try to answer the question: why does Brecht think that a 'demonstration of this sort can serve as a satisfactory basic model of major theatre'?

▶ Read the extract from *Their Theatre and Ours* (Part 3, pages 76–78). How does it use some of the techniques Brecht advocates?

▶ Identify the Brechtian elements in the extract from *Oh, What a Lovely War!* (Part 3, pages 81–83). What effect do they have?

Pinter's early plays

The late 1950s and the 1960s were decades that have become linked with the growth of material prosperity. Harold Macmillan, who was Prime Minister from 1957 to 1963, made the statement: 'Most of our people have never had it so good.' It is true that the prosperity of this period can be measured in terms of growing wages, a developing taste for holidays abroad and the sale of domestic appliances from vacuum cleaners to televisions. But there was an undercurrent of anxiety, and also of a 'bitter almost inarticulate rage'.

Pinter was the representative playwright of the period. When asked what his plays meant, he famously replied: 'The weasel beneath the cocktail cabinet.' It was the critic, Harold Hobson, who put best the sense of lurking unease that is felt in Pinter's early work, from *The Room* (1957) to *The Birthday Party* (1958) and *The Caretaker* (1960):

> Mr Pinter has got hold of a primary fact of existence. We live on the verge of disaster. One sunny afternoon when Peter May is making a century at Lords against Middlesex, and the shadows are creeping along the grass, and the old men are dozing in the Long Room, a hydrogen bomb may explode. That is one sort of threat. But Mr Pinter's is of a subtler sort. It breathes in the air. It cannot be seen, but it enters the room every time the door is opened. There is something in your past — it does not matter what — which will catch up with you ...
>
> (*Theatre in Britain*, 1984)

Pinter and verse drama

When theatre audiences saw *The Birthday Party* for the first time, its originality baffled them and the play faced critical rejection. What made the play so puzzlingly original was partly Pinter's refusal to give characters the kind of past history which explained them to the audience. Who were the two strangers who came unexpectedly to the seaside boarding house? Who is Stanley, the unshaven lodger, and what is his relationship with the men? Are they figures from his past? It is not that Pinter provided no answers to these questions: the problem is that he provided too many. The past that defined character and cleared up the plot in the plays of Ibsen, Shaw or Rattigan had become uncertain, and with the loss of that certainty, the whole world of Pinter's plays became stranger and more menacing.

It was not only the characters' lack of an agreed past that puzzled Pinter's first audience and critics: it was also a lack of sense of genre. At first, the opening scene of *The Birthday Party* looks as if it is set for comedy with the inanities of the dialogue between husband and wife (see Part 2, page 65), but as the strangers begin to take over the household and victimise Stanley, the menace builds up. Laughter in Pinter is always uneasy.

The battle for survival was the underlying theme not only of *The Birthday Party*, but also of *The Caretaker* and *The Homecoming* (1965). (There is an extract from *The Homecoming* in Part 3, pages 83–84). In each play an outsider comes in to a fixed family setting and disturbs the fragile equilibrium of relationships. Pinter's picture of society is of a ruthless battle for territory and power. The battle is often waged in the language of veiled politeness or the commonplace, but contains beneath its surface a message of aggression or lust. (See also Part 2, page 66 on sub-text.) Pinter makes the audience do what they do in real life: ask questions about the truthfulness of the words people use, about whether a speaker may be disguising, hiding or shading the truth. As in real life, words are rarely neutral: they are the weapons people use to survive and maintain their position. They are as likely to conceal as to reveal. As words are questionable, so too are Pinter's characters who are at bottom mysterious and unknowable:

> A character on stage who can present no convincing argument or information as to his past experience, his present behaviour or his aspirations, nor give a comprehensive analysis of his motives, is as legitimate and as worthy of attention as one who, alarmingly, can do all these things. The more acute the experience the less articulate its expression.
>
> (quoted in William Baker and Stephen Ely Tabachnick
> *Harold Pinter*, 1973)

T.S. Eliot had looked forward to a poetic drama in the 1930s and 1940s but, with a few exceptions, it did not happen. The language of the theatre remained resolutely prose, but what did develop in the hands of Pinter and others, was a highly charged prose that shared much of the rhythm, the density and suggestiveness of poetry.

▶ Read the extract from *Landscape* (Part 3, pages 86–87). How does Pinter create two very different voices here? Examine the use of pause, silence and repetition.

▶ With this extract in mind, how far do you agree that prose drama cannot express the moments of greatest intensity? Are there any other moments from plays that you know which you could bring into this discussion?

Arnold Wesker: the *Roots* trilogy

Arnold Wesker's trilogy, *Chicken Soup with Barley*, *Roots* and *I'm Talking About Jerusalem* (1958–1960), broke new ground. It presents the life of the Kahns, a working class Jewish family in the East End of London, and encompasses the political life of a generation. It begins in 1936 with fascist Blackshirts marching through the East End and deals with the Spanish Civil War, the Second World War and the Holocaust. It ends in 1960 with the failed attempt of the daughter of the family to set up a kind of rural socialism in Norfolk. In the ambitious scope of its plot, the trilogy tells the political history of Britain from 1936 to 1960 through the eyes of a Jewish family. Wesker's sense of the relationship between politics and the family and individual values underpinned his whole work.

Unlike his Marxist contemporary, Edward Bond, Wesker had no clear political allegiance. He often saw both sides of issues with a humanity sometimes seen as weakness by those who want theatre to serve a clearer political agenda. This is made clear in the powerful ending of *Chicken Soup with Barley* when Ronnie, shaken and disillusioned by the Russian invasion of Hungary, accuses his mother of betraying him by giving him a false ideal of communism.

RONNIE   *[rising, opens his eyes and shouts]* You know that I'm right. *You've* never been right about anything. You wanted everybody to be happy but you wanted them to be happy your way. It was strawberries and cream for everyone – whether they liked it or not. And now look what's happened. The family you always wanted has disintegrated, and the great ideal you always cherished has exploded in front of your eyes. But you won't face it. You just refuse to face it. I don't know how you do it but you do – you just do. *[Louder]* You're a pathological case, Mother – do you know that? You're still a *communist.*
[He wants to take back his words but he has lost the power to express anything any more.]

Wesker at his best gives a powerful sense that both his characters and their politics matter to him, but the tone is exploratory rather than didactic.

▶ Look at the extract from *Roots* (Part 3, pages 79–81) and examine how Wesker dramatises this moment. You might consider what exactly Beatie is attacking, the response of her family, what it might mean, and the use of Norfolk dialect.

1968

In 1968 the university students of Paris went onto the streets and were joined by trade unionists and workers to overthrow the government. In America, students objecting to the Vietnam War made increasingly violent protests and were confronted by armed police at the Democratic convention in Chicago. In Czechoslovakia, Russian tanks rolled into the capital, Prague, to suppress the democratic movement that had taken control in the 'Prague Spring'. The forces of the young seemed poised to strike against what they saw as authoritarian governments: revolution was in the air.

It was not only a political revolution that concerned the young. It was a social and sexual one too. The availability of the contraceptive pill allowed women to have more control of their sexual lives without fear of pregnancy, and legislation made abortions easier to obtain. Fashion expressed this new found freedom, as the designs of Mary Quant, the first boutiques and Carnaby Street helped to create the images of 'swinging' London. The mini skirt became the badge of modernity; ethnic clothes, bangles and beads expressed the revolt against developed consumerism in favour of a simpler way of life. Long hair was a mark of dissent and the American musical protesting against the Vietnam War was appropriately called *Hair* (1968). This was the era of the Beatles and the Rolling Stones, and the mood of the moment was best captured in some of the songs of the day. Joan Baez's 'We Shall Overcome' became an anthem of the protest movement and the Beatles' song, 'All You Need is Love', expressed the pacifism of flowerpower. The hippie had arrived.

In the theatre 1968 spelled the end of censorship. The presence of the censor, the Lord Chamberlain, had been an irritant to dramatists throughout the century. The abolition of censorship had several important consequences. Matters of religion and politics could be much more openly discussed. There was a new freedom to express sexual matters: homosexuality could at last be discussed rather than implied, and nudity on stage became legal.

The immediate result of the abolition of censorship was a production of the previously banned *Saved* (1965) by Edward Bond, and on-stage nudity in the love-rock musical *Hair*. However, the long term effect was the possibility of creating improvised scripts and developing them. This became the working method of many companies that followed in the tradition of the Unity theatre of the 1930s. Much of the drama of the 1970s had its roots in these collaborative fringe or alternative companies. Joint Stock pioneered 'workshopping', in which cast and writer would research a theme together and the play emerged from these sessions. Caryl Churchill worked on many of her plays with Joint Stock. David Edgar founded the General Will, and David Hare helped to found Portable Theatre. Many scripts like *Lay-by* (1968) and *Brassneck* (1973), for example, were collaborative and the companies' democratic organisation was an image of the kind of society they looked forward to. New performance spaces replaced the West End theatres and studios, halls, attics and pubs became regular venues.

Many of the groups felt that touring was a necessary part of the agenda of the new drama. John McGrath founded 7:84 in 1971 to tour socialist plays throughout

Britain. In 1973, the Scottish section broke away and had an immediate success with its account of the exploitation of the oil industry in *The Cheviot, the Stag, and the Black, Black, Oil*. **Community theatre** took drama to the local communities: Ann Jellicoe organised pageants in Dorset; Peter Cheeseman worked on social documentary theatre in Stoke on Trent. Touring companies like ATC and Cheek by Jowl owed their origins to this movement.

Feminist groups began to emerge in the early 1970s. The Women's Theatre Group was founded in 1973 and, in 1975, Monstrous Regiment grew from Joint Stock. Black and Asian theatre also had its beginnings in the late 1960s and early 1970s, aiming to establish theatre companies that were independent of white control and to represent the black experience. The African theatre company Temba was founded, as was Tara Arts, reflecting the Asian community. During the 1970s and 1980s many more groups were formed. These companies developed from making social statements to producing mainstream and challenging works such as Tara Arts' *Scenes in the Life of …* (1982) which told the story of a young Asian immigrant, and adaptations of classics, for example, setting Gogol's *The Government Inspector* in India.

In the excitement of 1968 there was the buzz of change: young dramatists examining new kinds of theatre in new spaces encouraging new audiences.

Edward Bond

Edward Bond set out to write for what he called a 'Rational Theatre'. This meant, in part, a theatre that set itself up against the theatre of the absurd. For Bond, theatre is the servant of a Marxist or socialist analysis of society. It is less about the individual, more about society. It should not strive towards **catharsis**, but towards analysis and social action.

'I write about violence as naturally as Jane Austen wrote about manners', wrote Bond in his Preface to his play *Lear* (1971). Violence does indeed run through the whole of Bond's work, because he sees it as endemic in a class society run on a capitalist basis. The cycle of the bully and the bullied endlessly repeating their roles, is Bond's view of capitalism. Bond was the most revolutionary voice in British theatre of the 20th century: '… from the political viewpoint, I would have thought there is no ambivalence in my plays at all … I think that there is no viable political system in existence in the world at the moment … Far from ensuring prosperity and happiness, most systems are actually vicious …' Bond wrote in a letter.

The extract from *Saved* (1965) in Part 3 (pages 84–86) is not, as might appear, a piece of especially grim naturalism, but a deliberate attempt to shock an audience from its complacency and to make them leave the theatre with a sense of the need for urgent action. Bond, whose theatre has much in common with that of Brecht, called his method here 'the Aggro technique'.

As he has developed as a playwright, Bond has experimented widely with dramatic forms from the early naturalism of *Saved*, to the pantomime treatment of Queen Victoria in *Early Morning* (1968), rewriting Shakespeare in *Lear* and the apocalyptic vision of life after a nuclear holocaust in *The War Plays* (1985).

▶ Read the extract from *Saved* (Part 3, pages 84–86). Examine how the scene builds up. What is the significance and dramatic point of the park bell ringing? What effect do Pam's final words have? Does this episode represent an argument for censorship in your view?

▶ In the Author's Note to the play Bond wrote: 'Clearly the stoning to death of a baby in a London park is a typical English understatement. Compared to the strategic bombing of German towns it is a negligible atrocity, compared to the cultural and emotional deprivation of most of our children its consequences are insignificant.'

How here is Bond demonstrating his idea of 'the Rational Theatre'? Do you agree with him?

▶ Read Brecht's account of epic theatre in Part 4, page 107. From your reading, how does this account illuminate your reading of the extract from *Saved*?

David Edgar

Whereas Bond's theatre uses parable, poetry and symbol, Edgar's is based on the journalism he learned before becoming a playwright. The description of his role as a dramatist that he favoured most was based on that of the critic Michael Billington: 'a secretary for the times through which I am living', Edgar's plays are based directly on social and political events of the second half of the 20th century. His early work springs from the agit-prop work he did for the touring group, the General Will, in which shows were written quickly to attack particular political targets, for example, the Housing Finance Act in his play, *Rent, or Caught in the Act* (1972). The material was topical and the style fast-moving.

Destiny

Political theatre of this kind dated as the issue dated, and in the play *Destiny* (1976) Edgar moved from propaganda to a deeper analysis of British politics. The way that history shapes individuals and politics is central to Edgar's thought. *Destiny* takes as its theme the growth of a far right political party called Nation Forward. The play was immediately topical: race had been a leading issue in the West Bromwich by-election, and the Conservative Party was divided by the speeches of Enoch Powell, whose phrase 'rivers of blood' is echoed in the imagery of the play.

The distinctive quality of Edgar's analysis of politics can be seen in the epic structure of the play that begins in India on the day of independence in 1947, and spans 30 years, following its characters back to Britain where the Colonel becomes a Tory MP, the young Sikh, Khera, becomes a factory worker, and the Sergeant the local Forward Party candidate.

The theme of the play is fascism. Major Rolfe returns to Northern Ireland to mourn his dead son who has been shot by a sniper's bullet. He speaks directly to the audience holding a crumpled Union Jack which he 'cradles … as he would a baby'. Rolfe, speaking about his dead son, demands sympathy. Yet his grief has been channelled into a general hatred that links the IRA, immigration to Bradford, the Bristol race riots and racial tension in Birmingham. Edgar lays bare the roots of fascism in the anger of the powerless father, and the way that specific issues become general paranoia. Its appeal is not to the mind but to the 'gut'. By the end of the speech, Rolfe has changed the bundle that he cradled to a flag raised in patriotic salute. Stage darkness falls as he looks to a Hitlerian 'iron dawn'. The complexity of audience response is far from the simplicities of agit-prop. The audience must watch with appalled sympathy the transition from a patriot mourning a dead child to a fascist salute. So Edgar's political theatre is not one of slogans and simplifications but probingly complex.

The final scene of *Destiny* is set in a room in a London merchant bank. A dark picture of the putting down of the Indian Mutiny links the scene thematically to the opening. Cleaver, the dominant fascist thinker, has succeeded in gaining promises of financial support for his party and asks at the end of the play: 'What can stop us now?'

	Suddenly lights change. CLEAVER *and* TURNER *lit from behind, in silhouette. A* VOICE *is heard; gentle, quiet, insistent. It is the voice of* ADOLF HITLER.
ADOLF HITLER	Only one thing could have stopped our Movement: if our adversaries had understood its principle, and had smashed, with the utmost brutality, the nucleus of our new Movement.
	Slight pause.
HITLER	Nuremburg. Third of September 1933.
	Blackout.

This is a climactic and shocking ending, but its very surprise makes the audience examine what is going on around them. The true force behind, and inspiration of, the party is revealed first as big business, then as Hitler himself. As the audience could hear the National Front noisily demonstrating against the play during its first performances, the threat must have seemed all the more terrifyingly real. What the audience could now do was to be aware. The final message of the play is that there is no such thing as destiny – only individuals who can change history if they are not duped.

David Hare

David Hare's work runs parallel to Edgar's. Both dramatists were born just after the Second World War; both have held strongly left wing views; both started writing agit-prop plays for companies they helped to found (the General Will in Edgar's case; Portable Theatre in Hare's) and both developed to write for the wider stages of the theatre (Edgar for The Royal Shakespeare Company and Hare for the National). Ultimately, however, they are very different: Edgar has some hope for change, whether it comes from the Greenham Common women at the end of *Maydays* (1983) or the political awareness his plays give, but Hare's plays are based on satirical mockery and despair. If there is to be a new Jerusalem. it is up to the audience to infer it.

Hare's early plays show the influence of agit-prop in the simplicity of their characterisation and their desire to shock and challenge an audience. Characteristically Hare chooses a genre and then subverts it. *Brassneck* (1973) is the family saga of the Bagley dynasty who arrive apparently penniless in a Midland town and soon take over all its institutions. But this study of generational power is not in the mould of a rags-to-riches story, for the tone is at once savage and complex. The final scene is set in the nightclub owned by Sidney, called The Lower Depths. It illustrates the power and vigour of this bitter comedy. The guests at the nightclub are all the political bigwigs, Labour and Conservative, who have helped Bagley and his family to power and who have profited by his rise. Sidney has proposed that they should join together to market the ultimate profit-making drug – Chinese heroin. A stripper removes her costume of mayoral robes, and as the climax to her act:

> *The naked stripper fixes, then raises her hypodermic. Fanfare. End of strip. The curtains on the small stage close. The band stops playing. Stage lights to dazzling brightness.*
>
> SIDNEY   As Head of a great English Family I give you all a toast. The last days of capitalism.
> *They lift their glasses in silence. The floor slowly gives way beneath them, and they descend as the lights fade and they are swallowed up.*

These are bold expressionistic techniques – but the world of mediaeval drama and its subterranean Hell beneath the stage is also present.

Plenty (1978) acted as a kind of turning point between Hare's agit-prop work and the more recent work in which he has allowed characters to speak for themselves, working as editor and shaping the material. Its ironic title points to the post-war contrast between material plenty and spiritual dearth. At the moral centre of the play is Susan Traherne, who finds in wartime an excitement and a sense of exhilaration that she cannot replicate in peacetime. Hare creates a complex heroine who is both the moral conscience of the play, seeking a way to live honourably in a country that has betrayed its wartime past, and a hysterical drug addict. When the actress playing Susan said to Hare after a performance: 'What a waste!' Hare added, 'But what a glory!'

Hare reclaims the Second World War from the film stereotype 'which was simply an opportunity for the British to behave with monotonous courage', and treats the Suez crisis as a centrally important betrayal of honour. *Plenty* has an epic sweep and a breadth of theme, which covers the decline of hope in post-war Britain, conveyed through an intensely realised and complex heroine.

After *Plenty* Hare wrote a trilogy of plays dealing with the state of the nation. Beginning with *Racing Demon* in 1990, which took as its theme the Church of England, Hare turned to the judiciary in *Murmuring Judges* (1991) and the world of politics in *The Absence of War* (1994). In these plays his dramatic method is based on detailed research into the world he deals with. Political theatre has become for Hare much closer to the work of a journalist, reporting the reality of the issues through the voices of those involved. Indeed, in his one-man play *Via Dolorosa* (1998), Hare dramatised the conversations he had had with Palestinians and Israelis on a visit to the Middle East to create a picture of that conflict. It is their passionate and conflicting voices in Hare's head that constitute the play.

▶ Read the extract from *Amy's View* (Part 3, pages 94–95) and discuss the way that Hare brings the discussion about the merits of theatre to life. How far is this a neutral presentation of an argument and how far is does it show a bias?

The 1970s and 1980s

The promised revolution never came and two Labour Governments, led by Harold Wilson and James Callaghan (1964-1970 and 1974-1979), failed to deliver the profound social change that so many of the political dramatists hoped for. The real focus of change during these years was not political but social, as women's liberation challenged traditional stereotypes of women. Germaine Greer published *The Female Eunuch* (1970) which described marriage as the legal enslavement of women. The women's liberation movement began to question the role of women as child rearers and homemakers. The movement also had a strongly activist element, for example, throwing smoke and stink bombs to disrupt the 1970 Miss World competition. In the same year, the Women's Street Theatre Group was formed.

Margaret Thatcher became Prime Minister in 1979. Under her leadership the Conservatives ruled Britain throughout the 1980s. The 'revolution' that so many on the left had imagined, turned out to be a right wing one. 'Thatcherism' became a shorthand term for her particular style of Conservative rule. Although 'Thatcherism' was particularly associated with economic theory, it also had a strong moral component. The keynote of Mrs Thatcher's conservatism was a defence of individual freedom. She attracted powerful popular support and equally powerful hostility. What happened in the 1980s was, according to the historian Peter Clarke, the creation of a more divided society: 'By any test from statistical surveys of relative incomes to the striking appearance of beggars on the street, Britain became a more unequal society.' On one side was the City with its young traders able to make huge sums of money after the financial deregulation known as the Big Bang in 1986, and on the other the poor and the deprived in the inner cities. Caryl Churchill's *Serious Money* (1987), expressed the hostility of many dramatists to the 'yuppies' and the materialistic values of the 1980s in a satire on the stock market. It ended on the chorus:

> These are the best years of our lives, and as we toast
>   the blushing bride
> My Maserati has arrived, join hands across the great
>   divide

BACK UP   *fiddle diddle iddle etc.*
CHORUS   Five more glorious years, five more glorious years
B/U   we're saved from the valley of tears for five more
glorious years
pissed and promiscuous, the money's ridiculous
send her victorious for five fucking morious
five more glorious years

Women playwrights

'Something new did emerge in British political life at the end of the 1970s … a sense that the emergent social issues were not to be constrained within the iron determinism of class politics, but were to be found within the much more fragile, porous but intriguing geology of difference. So the third wave of new playwrights – those who emerged in the early to mid 1980s – didn't answer to names like David, John and Howard but to names like Sarah, Bryony, Louise and Clare. In 1979 there were two currently-writing nationally-known women playwrights in Britain (Pam Gems and Caryl Churchill). Ten years later there were two dozen, whose work had dominated the decade.' So wrote David Edgar in 1999

Feminist theatre of a radical kind came from groups like the Women's Theatre Group (1973) and Monstrous Regiment (1975) for which Caryl Churchill wrote

Vinegar Tom (1976) and *Top Girls* (1982). At the beginning of the 1970s there was a tremendous exhilaration as women shared a sense of the importance of being part of a social and dramatic movement that could transform society. Gillian Hanna, one of the founder members of Monstrous Regiment, expressed the views of many:

> The atmosphere of the time was extraordinary: the shivering excitement in the air was almost tangible. Women felt they were throwing off the shackles of a thousand years or more and finding freedom. ... We were going to change things irrevocably, and our daughters and granddaughters would be able to learn from our successes and mistakes. Somehow we would pass on our knowledge, so that the next generation could take up where we left off instead of having to start all over again.
>
> (Introduction to *Monstrous Regiment*, 1991)

What this meant for the stage was articulated in Monstrous Regiment's aims in 1975:

> To produce great shows
> To discover and encourage women writers
> To explore a theory of feminist culture. 'What is a feminist play?'
> To resurrect women's 'hidden history'.
> To give women opportunities for work – especially in technical areas, which had always been male preserves.
> To put *real* women on the stage. No more stereotypes ...

The impact of the women writers has been to change the cultural geography. Some writers explored the mother-daughter relationship; others examined sexual relationships, and a significant number rewrote history as 'her story' and shed light on the 'hidden history' of women. Just as Beatie found her own feminine and regional Norfolk voice at the end of *Roots* (see the extract in Part 3, pages 79–81), so many women came to find their own distinctive voices that had long been concealed by a male establishment of writers and directors. Many plays were written for all-women casts and all-women theatre companies were formed. What began as a protest became an artistic movement with a kind of pioneering vitality. The influence it has had is not confined to women's theatre, but has transformed the representation of gender or gender politics on stage generally.

Caryl Churchill

Caryl Churchill's career illustrates the development of women's theatre. Her work developed from roots established in working with Joint Stock and Monstrous

Regiment. Her plays link her feminism with a socialist view on society – women are often seen as an underclass to be possessed or used by men. *Owners* (1972), the play that made her reputation at the Royal Court, reversed the stereotype of the dominant man and the passive woman. Its heroine, Marion, is a go-getting landlord who attempts to evict a young couple from her property and then cheats the young mother, Lisa, into signing adoption papers that give away her own child. In her monstrous selfishness, she is a prototype for Marlene in *Top Girls*.

Her husband, Clegg, is a butcher, in every sense, and more than matches Marion in his monstrosity, but ownership for him is the control of women. After seducing Lisa he says:

> I didn't say you could get up. You won't be suitable unless you lie flat, did you know that, very feminine and do just as you're told. On your back and underneath is where I like to see a lady. And a man on top. Right on top of the world. Because I know what you ladies like. You like what I give you. I didn't say you mustn't move at all. But just in response.

This is distinctive of Caryl Churchill's wit: it makes its points in a satirical way, building up a comic caricature of Clegg and allowing him to damn himself.

The play is built on the opposition of capitalism to a kind of eastern passivity represented by Marion's tenant, Alec – an opposition that can take financial or sexual or gender forms. The treatment of these issues as black farce and the sexual confusions owed something to Joe Orton's *Entertaining Mr Sloane*, but the humour has more satirical and political bite.

In *Top Girls* Marlene marks her promotion to managing director of the Top Girls agency by throwing a party to which are invited a number of famous and mythical women from the past. The first act celebrates her achievement and that of the other women (see the extract in Part 3, pages 88–90). All the women are in one sense strong survivors and all have lost children.

The second act is a stark contrast to the opulence of the restaurant, as the action moves to a children's shelter in a back yard which Angie and her friend have made into a den. It slowly emerges that the slightly retarded Angie is Marlene's daughter, not her niece. She has been brought up as her sister Joyce's child. The final scene presents the argument between the two sisters as they review the consequences of their actions. Joyce has stayed where she was born and looks after Angie and her ageing mother. Marlene has devoted her life to her career, had two abortions, and rarely communicated with her family. In this conversation about men at the end of the play, personal and political issues are intertwined:

MARLENE	Who needs them? Well I do. But I need adventures more. So on on into the sunset. I think the eighties are going to be stupendous.
JOYCE	Who for?
MARLENE	For me / I think I'm going up up up.
JOYCE	Oh for you. Yes, I'm sure they will.
MARLENE	And for the country, come to that. Get the economy back on its feet and whoosh. She's a tough lady, Maggie. I'd give her a job. / She just needs to hang in there.

Against this vision is her sister's sense of wasted lives: 'nothing's changed for most people'. The lonely disoriented daughter has the last word in the play: 'Frightening'.

Caryl Churchill's plays question rather than come to conclusions. In *A Light Shining in Buckinghamshire* (1976) she questions the possibility of radical change in society by examining the English Civil War. In *Cloud Nine* (1979) she examines possible different sexual relationships in the days of the Empire and today. In *Top Girls* the issues are to do with success and the price of success for women.

Just as distinctive as her subject matter is Churchill's radical and inventive approach to dramatic form. No two plays are remotely alike for she is constantly experimental in her dramatic technique. She uses song in *Vinegar Tom* (1976), verse drama for the satire on the City in *Serious Money* (1987), and in *The Skriker* (1993), produced with the dance company Second Stride, all the words are sung to present a nightmarish fairy story.

▶ Read the extract from *Top Girls* (Part 3, pages 88–90). What effect does Churchill's use of the technique of overlapping dialogue have?

▶ How far could you relate this treatment of Marlene's success to the commercial values of the 1980s and to ideas of feminism?

Pam Gems

Pam Gems' sense of feminism is a contrasting one, lacking the political dimension of Churchill's. She came to prominence with *Dusa, Fish, Stas and Vi* (1976), which takes as its subject four liberated young women sharing a London flat. Outwardly the four women are very different. Dusa, in the process of a divorce, is terrified as her ex-husband flees abroad with their young children; Fish is a middle class feminist, an activist for women's rights ('We make the choices. The right to take decisions about our own lives is one we have to fight for. It's one we have to win.'). Stas works as a physiotherapist by day and as a prostitute by night to pursue her ambition of becoming a marine biologist and Vi, 'a very thin redhead', refuses food. The play explores with humanity the difficulties and contradictions these women have with the different roles they have chosen, or are called upon to play.

The end of the play reaches towards an apparently happy, even sentimental, climax. It is Fish's birthday, the children are about to be reunited with their mother Dusa, and Vi makes a splendid comic entrance as a traffic warden giving the sleeping Fish her first ticket. But Fish is not asleep: she has killed herself and the last words of the play are her suicide note: 'My loves, what are we to do? We won't do as they want any more, and they hate it. What are we to do?' The play asks questions about the new roles of 'liberated women' and their emotional consequences.

It is this humane questioning of the roles women play in a man's world which Gems' next plays explored. Gems is specially drawn to achievers who make successes of their public lives: *Queen Christina* (1977), *Piaf* (1978) and *The Blue Angel* (1991) all take successful women as their subjects. In *Piaf* Gems shows how her heroine could rise above a background of abuse and neglect to become a great singer through her own toughness and vitality. This self-expression is also the theme of *The Blue Angel* in which another chanteuse literally finds her own voice in a performance role. It is through the power of their art that these women triumph over adversity.

In *Loving Women* (1984), the revolutionary Frank has been living with Susannah for five years but has taken up with Crystal, a young hairdresser. Whereas Susannah is middle class, dowdily intellectual and feminist, Crystal dresses up as Marilyn Monroe for Frank when she is not providing stodgy suppers for him.

In the final act, however, ten years later in 1983, all positions have altered. Frank has now been married to Crystal for ten years and they have had two children. The marriage is on the rocks. Crystal has discovered infidelity, along with commercial success as a West End hair stylist. Frank has reverted to his revolutionary past just as Susannah returns from social work in Bolivia, disillusioned with revolutionary politics. Her values have become family values and her only wish is to have a child.

Loving Women is a sharp comedy of ironic reversals as characters' positions and attitudes change with the times. The questions the play asks are about what women want to be, how men and women are to get on together and how children are to be brought up in an age when 'everything's collapsed'. The final suggestion is that Frank, Crystal and Susannah live together. In a tentative ending as the two women plot their future, Frank has left angrily. Will he return? Will they set up home together successfully?

Women's voices

Pam Gems' plays put women at the centre of their action, showing the pressures and social consequences of the changing sense of women's roles, of sexual and family patterns. They present a sympathetic and detailed balance sheet of social change. They have encouraged many young women writers to look to their own experience as women for the subject matter of their plays. Sharman Macdonald's *When I Was a Girl I Used to Scream and Shout* (1984) brings a young girl's sexual and emotional awakening to the stage, and Charlotte Keatley's *My Mother Said I Never Should* (1987) deals with four generations of mother-daughter relationships.

Sarah Daniels represents a much more radical feminist view. In *Masterpieces* (1983) she shows the effect of pornography on one woman. Having seen some especially violent images from so-called 'snuff' movies in which the woman is eventually killed, the heroine, Rowena, pushes an unknown commuter off a platform into the path of an oncoming tube train. She is then examined unsympathetically by a male psychiatrist and sentenced by a male judge who refuses to take into account her defence:

> One thing is indisputable. A man has lost his life as the direct consequence of the action taken against him by you. A man whom you have admitted you never met before, I would suggest to you that the evidence you have put forward is nothing more than an irrelevant fabrication to further some fanatical belief that the laws concerning pornography in this country are inadequate. But that is of no concern here.

At the end of the play, Rowena discusses the violence done to women by men, with a policewoman who has seen it all:

> I don't want anything to do with men who have knives or whips or men who look at photos of women tied and bound, or men who say relax and enjoy it. Or men who tell misogynist jokes.
> *Blackout*.

This was angrily extreme theatre, and it made its point through strong images and characterisation that neared caricature. In its lumping together of jokes about women with sexual violence, it mounted a forceful attack on men without examining other sides of the issue. This dramatic technique was typical of what was called in the 1970s 'the aggro effect', and the play succeeded in arousing the strongest positive and negative reactions.

Timberlake Wertenbaker

Timberlake Wertenbaker dislikes the compound term 'women's playwriting', because writing such as hers lacks the distinctive focus on women that marked the more feminist plays of the 1980s.

Our Country's Good (1988) developed from an idea of reclaiming a little known history and used the workshop technique of research and improvisation. Of crucial importance was the visit to Wormwood Scrubs to see a play by Howard Barker. *Our Country's Good* is set, significantly, in 1789 at the time of the French Revolution. It is the account, based on historical evidence, of the transportation of a group of convicts to Australia. It is proposed that the convicts put on a play and there is a general discussion about theatre and what it is for (see the extract in Part 3, pages 92–94). A Restoration comedy, *The Recruiting Officer*, is chosen and the play follows the production from difficult beginnings, with a largely illiterate cast, to its triumphant first night. The production has changed everybody in ways that even the liberal and civic-minded Governor had not imagined. Ralph, the play's director, discovers himself in the love scenes, the self-effacing and shy Mary becomes the 'brave and strong' heroine, Sylvia. Liz, who has been wrongly accused of stealing and condemned to death, finds in the eloquence of her part in the play her own voice to confront her accusers. In the introduction to her collected plays, Wertenbaker wrote about how the violence in her next play *The Love of the Nightingale* (1988) 'erupts in societies when they have been silenced for too long', adding, 'Without language brutality will triumph.' It is the experience of the language of the theatre that transforms the individual convicts and their society in *Our Country's Good*: 'In that play, I wanted to explore the redemptive power of the theatre, of art, for people who had been silenced.' The play begins with the building of a gallows that is described as the colony's theatre, a theatre of retribution and savagery; it ends with the applause of an audience at a more truly civilised spectacle, the performance of *The Recruiting Officer*.

The play has another perspective – that of the Aborigine whose brief poetic scenes punctuate the play's structure. At first, the colonists seem to him to be part of the Aboriginal myth of the past, dreamtime, but in his final words he describes their legacy, smallpox, the western disease that left the Aborigines helpless:

> Look: oozing pustules on my skin, heat on my forehead. Perhaps we have been wrong all this time and this is not a dream at all.

Just as one possibility of redemption is offered to the colonists of Australia, their arrival spells death and disease to its native inhabitants.

► The critic Janet Brown identified four common features of feminist drama:

1 the sex role reversal
2 the presentation of historical figures as role models
3 satire of traditional sex roles
4 the direct portrayal of women in oppressive situations.

How far, and to what effect, have you noted the use of these features in your reading of women's drama?

Joe Orton

In the 1930s, farce enjoyed enormous popularity at the Aldwych Theatre in London's West End and in the 1960s at the Whitehall with Brian Rix. When Joe Orton's *Entertaining Mr. Sloane* appeared in 1964, it challenged the comfortable views that farce often expressed. In conventional farce, after the mistakes of the night comes the day in which mistakes are unravelled, and life goes on. Orton's farces present a very different ending and embody a very different view of society.

In *Entertaining Mr. Sloane* shades of Pinter's influence can be seen in the plot and characterisation. Sloane is a young man who has been picked up in the public library and taken home by the middle-aged Kath, who invites him to be her lodger. Her brother Ed at first wants to get rid of him, but feels sexually attracted to Sloane and employs him as his driver. Kath is also attracted to Sloane and becomes pregnant by him. Sloane however is a murderer, and Kath's father a witness to the deed. When he begins to talk too much, Sloane murders him. The action of the play turns on the battle for possession of Sloane between brother and sister. Kath's trump card against her prosperous and powerful brother is that she will go to the police with her information unless she can keep her child and Sloane stays with her:

> ED   Go to the police then. What will you achieve? Nothing.
>   This boy was carried away by the exuberance of youth.
>   He's under age.
> KATH   You struck the Dadda down in cold blood Mr. Sloane. In
>   the course of conversations before his death he told me
>   one or two things of interest.

There is a real separation of language from dramatic action here. What is taken for granted is that the murder has no moral value at all: it is simply an instrument in the crudely selfish battle for possession, an instrument of moral blackmail. Kath talks the language of sentiment, always referring to her father as 'the dadda', but this is belied by what she is doing and by crude threats ('If you go I'll tell the police.'). Language is used by Orton to mask the real drives of power and sex: much of the distinctive quality of his savage humour comes from this disjunction of word and deed.

Orton's characters speak in all kinds of official and public voices, but he lacks Pinter's subtle sense of the depths beneath the verbal surface. His characters tend to move from one rhetorical stance to another. There is no sub-text. Orton's characters do not use language to make sense of the world and cannot know each other. They are lonely creatures forever at linguistic cross purposes.

In his last play, *What the Butler Saw* (1969), Orton developed the theme of madness and set the play in a private psychiatric clinic. In the clinic, Dr Prentice attempts to seduce a young woman, Geraldine Barclay, who has applied to be his secretary. His wife has also had a liaison, with the page of the Station Hotel. During the play, Geraldine is stripped of her clothes twice, put in a straitjacket and has her hair shaved. The motif of losing clothes is of course one of the staples of farce, but here Orton uses multiple variations on the theme, as characters have to dress and undress: the page wears a leopard-spotted dress and Geraldine dresses as a boy. The motif reaches its comic climax as, at the end of the play, 'the skylight opens, a rope ladder is lowered and, in a great blaze of glory, Sergeant Match, the leopard-spotted dress torn from one shoulder and streaming with blood, descends'. Dressing and cross-dressing are the images of the sexual confusion at the heart of the play.

In *What the Butler Saw*, Orton celebrated the vitality and variety of sexual behaviour: 'Love must bring greater joy than violence.' Orton looked back to a long tradition of farce as a release from inhibitions into a world of comic and erotic playfulness.

Through his plays Orton presents a comic and farcical anarchy in which the innocent suffer and the guilty thrive. All forces of order are corrupt. Violence and cruelty are never far from the surface, but at the end of *What the Butler Saw* there is a possibility of hope and escape from the mad world.

▶ Compare the endings of any comedies you have read with the endings of Joe Orton. How far do they resolve the issues of the play or end 'happily'?

▶ Compare the language of the extract from *The Homecoming* (Part 3, pages 83–84) with Orton's.

Alan Ayckbourn

If you write an honest picture of a person, sooner or later you're going to hit bedrock of frustration or disappointment or something. There's a tendency to dodge that when you begin. Farce is a tragedy that's been interrupted. All you do is edit it at the right point. If you let a character's life run on before editing – let's say until he's married ten years – then as a result you'll have a slightly darker, but I hope truer, picture.

> It seems to me that the deeper you go into a character, the sadder
> the play must inevitably become.
> (quoted in *File on Ayckbourn*, compiled by Malcolm Page, 1989)

In these remarks Alan Ayckbourn pinpointed his achievement: he writes a kind of comedy dealing with serious themes like loneliness, infidelity and death. It is characteristic of Ayckbourn to see how closely related are the issues of tragedy and comedy: 'I'd love to write a truly hilarious dark play.'

Orton created a very theatrical language that did not allow him to present sympathetic characters, whereas Alan Ayckbourn created a language that gives full expression to characters who strike an audience as familiar and comically human. He catches the exact tone of voice of his characters in a way that makes them seem so familiar and funny. Through his art, everyday language and commonplace speech become revealing. In *Time of My Life* (1992), for example, Laura receives a gift of a pair of earrings from her daughter-in-law for her 54th birthday:

LAURA	*[To STEPHANIE]* … they're so unusual. That's what I love about them. I don't think I've seen anything like them before. Not even in Crete.
STEPHANIE	No, as I say there's this woman we met at the nursery school, she's just started up. She's working from home but she's trained in jewellery making. She's fully trained. But she gave it up to have children but now they're at school she's just starting up again on her own from home …
LAURA	I've not seen anything like them anywhere. I think they're just lovely. I think I'll probably go to bed in them …
STEPHANIE	They suit you, I thought they'd suit you. They're your colour …

Ayckbourn is a remarkable theatrical craftsman. Each of his plays is an experiment with dramatic form. *The Norman Conquests* (1973) is a series of three plays based on the events of one weekend. The plays occur simultaneously so that each play happens in a particular room and 'one play is the off stage of another'. *Bedroom Farce* (1975) presents the audience with the events of three on-stage bedrooms and the inter-relationship of their occupants. The four scenes of *Just Between Ourselves* (1976) depicts four birthday parties in one garage, and in *Taking Steps* (1979) Ayckbourn sets his farce in a three-storey Victorian house squashed into the one level of the stage floor. To underline the theme of choice in *Sisterly Feelings* (1978), Ayckbourn allowed the cast to develop some scenes according to the toss of a coin and the actresses' wishes.

Ayckbourn turned to social themes in his *Small Family Business* (1987), in which a young man tries to run a family furniture firm on entirely ethical lines, but gets implicated with corruption on a large scale. Ayckbourn's own comments on the play are especially revealing about his future work. 'What the play is really about is the virtual non-existence of set moral codes any more, and the fallacy of trying to live by one. I think now the only thing we can do – and in a way cannot help doing – is to make up our own moral codes as we go along ...' Ayckbourn sees the same kind of material corruption in society as Bond and Hare did, but his response is a moral and personal, not a political, one: 'Political theatre is so busy being political that it forgets to be theatre.'

The theme of moral choice became a focus of Ayckbourn's playwriting. Ayckbourn's more mature characters take decisions based on a perception of reality: others are blinded to it by obsession, selfishness or fantasy. Ayckbourn has always been concerned with the allure and danger of fantasy: in *Woman in Mind* (1985) the heroine is unhappily married to a vicar and the play presents her fantasy world alongside the real one. Cyberspace offers escapism from reality in *Henceforward* (1987), where the hero rejects his wife and child for a female android. *Virtual Reality* (1999) became the title of Ayckbourn's 56th play. Alex Huby designs 'viewdows' which offer a view of his virtual reality garden and virtual reality gardener. His wife lives on the mobile phone and their son is imprisoned in his gadget-dominated room. All have chosen to be locked into their own fantasy worlds which lead to disaster. Ayckbourn defined tragedy as 'to do with decisions we make – wrong choices – leading to further wrong choices'.

Tom Stoppard

Stoppard's theatre is very different from the political dramatists of his generation, and from Orton and Ayckbourn in that he took his inspiration from literary and philosophical texts more than from the social and political context of his time.

In *Rosencrantz and Guildenstern Are Dead* (1964) Stoppard put into the foreground the two attendant lords of Shakespeare's *Hamlet* and made them the centre of the action. It is through their eyes that the plot of *Hamlet* unfolds. The plot of *Rosencrantz and Guildenstern* thus consists of the stories of Rosencrantz and Guildenstern and their relationships with the travelling players who are also on their way to Elsinore, with snippets from *Hamlet* acted out in the background.

The question is: who are these men? They are characters from a Shakespearean tragedy, victims of an action they do not understand. They are modern doubters, unsure of everything, even of which one of them is Rosencrantz and which Guildenstern. In their game playing, their waiting on a summons from a source they cannot understand, they have been compared to Beckett's two clowns in

Waiting For Godot. They may wear Elizabethan dress, but they are also our representatives looking through a modern idiom and perspective at the dramatic action of a play written 400 years ago, sometimes speaking directly to the audience. It is precisely this lack of settled identity that Stoppard uses to examine and question the sense of the fixed and the readily comprehensible.

When the audience watch *Rosencrantz and Guildenstern*, they are watching actors play travelling players playing parts in a play (*The Mousetrap*) within a play (*Hamlet*). This insetting of one play within the frame of another is characteristic of Stoppard's drama. But it is no mere clever trick, for through it Stoppard constantly asks the ultimate questions: what is reality and how can we know it?

Critics of Stoppard have sometimes seen him as a superficial joker, failing to engage with serious issues. *The Real Thing* (1982) was, in part, his answer to these charges. Brodie is a left wing political activist who makes a political protest against the presence of American missiles in Britain by burning a wreath on the steps of the Cenotaph. In prison he writes a play to express his views. Henry is a successful playwright who makes his living from writing, and here Stoppard opposes two ideas of what constitutes a play: the drama of propaganda and the drama of the commercial playwright.

Love and how it can be expressed is the main concern of *The Real Thing*. In the opening scene, Max discovers his wife's adultery when he finds the passport she has forgotten to take with her and discovers past lies:

> I notice that you never went to Amsterdam when you went to Amsterdam. I must say I take my hat off to you, coming home with Rembrandt place mats for your mother. It's those little touches that lift adultery out of the moral arena and make it a matter of style.

This sounds like the polished wit of Noel Coward, but it becomes apparent in the next scene that the opening is not 'real' but from Henry's latest play *House of Cards*. When the adultery and pain is real, as when Max discovers Annie's love affair with Henry, words fail him and he becomes incoherent. In the middle of a real love scene with Annie, Henry, the professional writer, finds he cannot write a love scene.

The Real Thing dramatises the difficulty of writing about love, as it stresses the power that love has over all the characters. The final irony is revealed only at the end of the play. Annie reveals that Brodie only set fire to the wreath to impress her because he had seen her on television: his politics were merely an expression of desire.

▶ Read the extract from *The Real Thing* (Part 3, pages 90–92) and consider the view of drama that Henry argues for. How far does Stoppard seem to endorse Henry's views? In what ways does Stoppard differ from any more obviously politically committed writer you have read?

When Stoppard came to write *Arcadia* in 1993, he was a master of the intricate plot which intertwined several stories together, often twisting the time scale, and challenged the audience to link them in order to find a pattern. The audience was put in the position of the Detective (a stage figure Stoppard often uses) in order to unravel the plot's meaning.

In *Arcadia* Stoppard achieved his most complex and resonant artistic form. The play is set in 'a very large country house in Derbyshire'. The time scale alternates between 1809 and today. How they relate to each other over time is a major theme of the play. *Arcadia* opens as the young Thomasina enquires from her tutor, 'What is a carnal embrace?' At the same time as finding out about love and desire, she is clearly asking some practical questions that lead directly to the kind of questions that are posed by modern physics:

> When you stir your rice pudding, Septimus, the spoonful of jam spreads itself round making red trails like the picture of a meteor in my astronomical atlas. But if you stir backward, the jam will not come together again. Indeed, the pudding does not notice and continues to turn pink just as before. Do you not think this is odd?

In *Arcadia* Stoppard used all the craft of the dramatist discussed in *The Real Thing*. Through the double time focus of the plot, Stoppard conveys both the passing nature of time in the initial contrast between the country house of 1809 and today, and the contrast between Regency and contemporary dress. In the final scene, the modern characters dress in Regency clothes for a photograph, and the audience sees a graceful dance from the Regency couple and an awkward one from the modern couple on the stage at the same time. This dramatic presentation insists on the recurring patterns of time, as well as its sequential nature. Stoppard uses a most expressive visual symbol for his theme of time in the table on which all the key objects have been left: by the end of the play, it has accrued a heap of significant objects, including a computer, geometrical solids, two portfolios and the Sunday papers.

It is a rare feat to write witty drama which embodies the speculations of abstract physics, but Stoppard and Michael Frayn in *Copenhagen* (1998) both broaden drama's horizons.

▶ What are the difficulties that may face a playwright trying to write about contemporary ideas? How have any playwrights that you have read dealt with abstract ideas in their plays?

Henceforward: the 1990s

Whilst established writers such as Ayckbourn, Churchill and Hare continued to develop, a new young crop of dramatists began to make their mark. The theatre historian and critic, Benedict Nightingale, wrote of their achievement:

> Starting in 1994, continuing through 1995 and 1996, a remarkable number of striking young playwrights emerged in England, mainly from the Royal Court's tiny Theatre Upstairs, and a pub-playhouse in West London, the Bush. Their ages ranged from twenty-two to thirty-four and they had much in common. Their characters drifted around weird cityscapes, where violence was a frequent threat and escape from feelings of entrapment mostly an illusion. But unlike their predecessors, these dramatists had no obvious ideology, no political credo, no social agenda. If their characters launched into generalisation, it was more likely to be about drugs or drink than the sins of the Establishment …
>
> But it's what one might dub the Theatre of Urban Ennui that most obviously expresses the feelings of a generation shaped by the 1980s. If one were to derive a capsule play from already performed work, it might involve gangs of girls adrift in a London where criminals dump bits of their rivals in plastic bags, rent boys are casually raped, there's a lively backstreet trade in stolen burglar alarms and voracious spivs gather beside ageing charabanc drivers dying of a surfeit of porn. These dramatists are stronger on character and situation than conflict, tension and structure, preferring to offer vivid snapshots rather than concoct plots, maybe because plot implies some coherence in people's lives. They relish the oddball, the misfit, the bizarre; but they are troubled by the helplessness and unhappiness they see all around. They are vastly entertaining yet they radiate moral concern. They are Mrs Thatcher's disoriented children.
>
> *(The Theatre, 1998)*

This is a neat, possibly too neat, summary of the work of many dramatists. No play since *Saved* has caused such uproar as Sarah Kane's *Blasted* (1995). Containing scenes of shocking violence, including homosexual rape, eye gouging and cannibalism, it attracted instant notoriety. Some critics also noted that the extremity of the action which brings the horrors of the conflict in Bosnia to a hotel room in Leeds is matched by a language of austere restraint. Extreme violence also featured in her next play *Cleansed* (1998), set in a university that has become a concentration camp, but there is also a hint of the power of love in the relationship of brother and sister. Kane's final work, before her suicide in 1999, was *Crave*

(1998) which was totally different in style. It is a poetic piece for four voices and like radio drama in that it consists in these four voices talking about despair and hopeless, obsessive love in a pared-down poetic language that owes a debt to Beckett and Eliot.

Mark Ravenhill's *Shopping and F***ing* (1006) links the sexual exploitation of the rent boy with the values of a society where everything is for sale, and the sexual violence of the play is part of its angry argument. Jez Butterworth's *Mojo* (1995), originally intended as a screenplay, takes as its theme the petty crooks of Soho in the mid-1950s and, in its black comedy treatment of their world, obscene language and romanticised violence, has been compared to the work of the film director, Quentin Tarantino. Whereas violence is linked to Kane's despair or to Ravenhill's anger, for Butterworth it is apparently taken for granted or meaningless.

Just as the 1980s saw an outburst of playwriting by and about women, so the 1990s saw an interest in the all-male and the gay play. Gay Sweatshop had been founded earlier in 1985 to encourage homosexual and lesbian theatre and Martin Sherman's *Bent* (1979) had controversially paralleled the persecution of homosexuals with the persecution of the Jews in the Holocaust. In the 1990s the focus was on the redefining of gender that women's writing had challenged men to do. Mark Ravenhill's *Handbag* (1999), for example, compares attitudes to parenthood and sexual behaviour at the beginning and at the end of the 20th century. Much of gay theatre was a response to the AIDS epidemic whose threat hung over the whole gay community. Kevin Elyot's *My Night with Reg* (1994) is a comedy about a promiscuous gay man with AIDS and how his friends deal with the crisis. *Beautiful Thing* (1994) by Jonathon Harvey gives young homosexual love in a housing estate in South London a conventionally romantic treatment, the only difference being that the couple are of the same sex. That homosexuality is seen as a relationship rather than an issue, showed a sense of progress and self-confidence that was justified by the play's success. The writer and actor William Ganimara wrote of all-men plays:

> So it's as if a lid is being lifted, or a stone is being turned, and we are given a slightly voyeuristic warts-and-all view of men in varying group situations parading both strengths and vulnerabilities, particularly vulnerabilities I think. And this gives the plays for the most part a common thread of self-criticism and self-examination which at the same time roots them very firmly in the 1990s in keeping with other genre writing, whether it's Nick Hornby writing about football or Blake Morrison writing about the death of his father
>
> (William Ganimara *State of Play* ed. David Edgar, 1999)

▶ Violence is very important in the playwriting (and films) of the last ten years. Why should this be so? Do you think there is any difference between violence staged (or in the cinema) and violence in a novel or poem? Compare and contrast the use of violence in any plays you have read.

Virtual reality

In Ayckbourn's play, *Virtual Reality* (1999), the hero is a designer of a virtual world who can look into a perfect virtual garden at a perfect virtual gardener. In Patrick Marber's *Closer* (1997) two characters, one pretending to be a woman, type furiously at their computer keyboards as one attempts to seduce the other by using pornographic chat. The whole of their conversation is projected onto a huge screen which dwarfs them. As one critic observed, the video screen is now as much a commonplace on stage as the French windows were in the 1930s. How will dramatists respond to the world of new technology? Will they look on its influence with the scepticism of Ayckbourn, the amusement of Marber, or will cinema and technology kill off the theatre as the film director, Dominic, argues in *Amy's View* in the extract in Part 3 (pages 94–95)?

Technology not only becomes part of the staging and subject matter, it also influences the idea of plot and character. Some modern playwrights owe a great debt to cinema and try to achieve the visual imagery, fast pace and slick editing of the film. Marber, for example, uses many of the technical devices of film: backtracking, varying focus and the split-shot image, and Butterworth's *Mojo* is cinematic in its pace and the way one scene dissolves into another. How should drama respond to the world of video and cinema? Should it try to ape cinematic effects or try to develop its own language?

Martin Crimp's *Some Attempts on her Life* (1997) deals with the theme of violence in a distinctive way. It dispenses with stage characters and clear narrative plot to present '17 scenarios for the theatre', or 'attempts', in order to give different versions of its heroine, Anne. (See the extract in Part 3, pages 96–97.) Anne appears to be a drowned daughter, killer and suicide, international terrorist and even a victim of aliens. (See also April de Angelis, Part 2, pages 68–69.) As in *Crave*, the voices that discuss Anne are unlocated and unnamed. Some may be Anne herself. In *Some Attempts on her Life* the audience has to make sense of the conflicting stories that the speakers tell about Anne and what happened to her. Gone is the reassurance of fixed stage character, gone too is the cause and effect plot development expressing a rational world.

The century ended as it began, with playwrights experimenting with dramatic form to challenge the audience to make sense of the world around them.

▶ Read the extract from *Amy's View* (Part 3, pages 94–95). How far do you agree with Dominic's point of view? What is the importance of film or technological change in the plays you have studied?

Assignments

1 Choose two passages from Part 3, one from each half of the 20th century. How does each passage reflect the dramatic concerns and conventions of its time?

2 Compare and contrast the ways in which two or three plays or extracts have treated social or political issues.

3 Write a short scene from a play in the style of one of the playwrights you have studied. This could be a parody if you wish. Add a detailed comment on how you tried to capture the individual quality and style of the playwright.

4 'Gender issues' and the relationship between the sexes have been a focus for much of 20th-century drama. Compare and contrast the treatment of these themes in two or three of the plays or extracts you have read.

2 | Approaching the texts

- What is the relationship between the text and dramatic performance?

- How does an understanding of genre, language use, characterisation and plot help to shape the interpretation of a play?

- What major theatrical movements have influenced playwrights?

Text and performance

Before there can be performance there normally has to be a text. A text is like a piece of genetic material in that it is capable of infinite multiplication. Unlike a gene, however, each of these performances will be uniquely different depending on the director, the staging, the actors and the audience.

There is no doubt that plays can be studied as literature and many famous critics have done exactly that. Indeed, there is a school of thought that would suggest the best productions of some plays are those inside the head rather than on the stage. The extreme opposite argument is that a play can only truly exist when it is in performance and that a detailed literary study of the text is limited and misleading.

Text and performance, however, may be seen to complement each other. An examination of the language of the text, patterns of imagery, plot and theme should inform any production. But the reading of the text should always be accompanied by a sense of the play in performance. The student of drama should be alert to all the nuances of language, but should also be directing an imaginary production in his or her head. This is the reason why it is so important to try to see as many productions as possible. Each production represents a new interpretation of the play to test against the text.

► When you have seen a production or video of a play that you have read, make brief notes of what struck you. How far did the production show you what you already knew, and how far did it challenge you to rethink?

Whose play is it?

The obvious answer to this question is: the playwright's. But, as discussed in the Introduction (page 6), a play is different from other forms of literature. Whereas a lyric poet can speak directly to the reader through the finished form of the poem, the dramatist has to invoke a director, a cast of actors, and some form of staging. This means that drama is essentially of a social or collaborative nature.

This argument has consequences if the question 'What is this play about?' is asked. It leads towards the view that a play's nature and meaning is shaped by many factors apart from the playwright's intention. This is why in drama, of all literary forms, context is crucial to understanding.

In addition, the notion of the meaning of a text being the same as the artist's intention has drawn a great deal of critical attention. This idea is known as the 'intentionalist fallacy'. It has been persuasively argued that the playwright is in no better position than anyone else to state the 'meaning' of his or her work, as there is no certain link between intention and outcome. Writers may well not be in the best position to judge their own work, and some critics have stressed the role of the unconscious in artistic creation. The extension of the intentionalist fallacy argument is to discard not only the writer's expressed views but also all forms of context, and to judge the work of art itself as self-sufficient and self-explanatory. The view may have merit as a corrective to biographical or social criticism that treats the play as a mere by-product of the author's life or circumstances. It is, however, an extreme position and is more relevant to the criticism of poetry than that of drama, because of the social nature of drama discussed above.

It does not follow, of course, that the dramatist's intention is irrelevant. On the contrary, it may prove to be vital evidence in understanding the play. The intention certainly cannot be ignored, but equally it is not the final word: it is up to you as audience and critic to decide how much weight to give it.

What kind of play is it?

A 17th-century audience going to see *Hamlet* would have known very clearly that they were watching a tragedy. They would also have known in broad terms what to expect: high language, serious matter and the death of a royal hero. An audience viewing a comedy would similarly know what kind of play to expect. This notion of fixed dramatic types lasted until the drama of the 1960s. Since then the notion of dramatic genres has become less clear, as playwrights have experimented with – and mixed – all kinds of forms to challenge the audience to respond to the new and the unpredictable. Nevertheless, a modern play may establish its genre very quickly by recognisable signposts, which may be those of setting or of language, and may thus set up a pattern of expectation.

▶ Look at the following play openings and the definition of genre in the glossary. Now try to see what genre each belongs to, and what audience expectations are set up.

> *By the factory wall at night.* JOSEF FRANK *alone.*
>
> FRANK   I don't sleep. I walk about London. So many people,

sleeping. Around you. For miles. After so many years, it is better to be tired. Not to think or remember. Ten million, asleep, around you, is warm. The ignorant English, like a warm overcoat. About me. It is better. While in the nightmare of the dark all the dogs of Europe bark.

*   *   *   *   *   *   *   *

BARRY *is in the pub playing darts*
BRENDA *comes in and goes to the bar*

BRENDA Hey mate. Can I have a drink on t'slate, eh. Summat on t'slate. I'm skint you see until me daughter gi's me some later. She comes in here, Carol, you know her. Gi' us one an' she'll pay you later. Eh. Eh. Go on lovey, gi'us a bottle. Oh sod off then. Stuck up flea. *[She turns round and sees* BARRY*]* Barry! Baz! Playin' darts then Baza?
He ignores her
What time is it Bar?

BARRY Dunno.

*   *   *   *   *   *   *   *

The dining room. Saturday 6pm … ANNIE *in baggy sweater, jeans and raffia slippers enters with a flower vase of water. She thumps this down in the middle of the table … gives the whole lot a final shake and that as far as she's concerned concludes her flower arrangement … when* SARAH *enters. She wears a light summer coat and dress. She is breathless.*

SARAH Hallo! We're here –
ANNIE Sarah!
SARAH *[embracing her]* Annie dear …
ANNIE Good journey?
SARAH Oh yes, yes, not bad. Reg drove far too fast as usual but we got here – oh, it's lovely to come down. I've been looking forward to this weekend away from it all for weeks. Weekend? It's barely a day. You've no idea how that dreary little house of ours gets me down.
ANNIE Oh it's not too bad.
SARAH Try living there sometime. Not a decent shop, not a cinema, not even a hairdresser except some awful place I can't go into because of the smell …

▶ Which of these passages was easier to place? Could you imagine the kind of plays that would develop from these beginnings?

The first is the opening of *Weapons of Happiness* (1973) by Howard Brenton and an example of epic realism. The second is the opening of *Road* (1986) by Jim Cartwright and its gritty dialogue might suggest naturalism or **kitchen sink drama**. The third is the opening of *Table Manners* by Alan Ayckbourn (1973) and even the title suggests that it is a **comedy of manners**.

So it is that a playwright may establish a genre and a mood almost immediately. Some playwrights, however, may not wish to. This is the beginning of *Fen* (1983) by Caryl Churchill:

> *As the audience comes in a boy from the last century, barefoot and in rags, is alone in the field, in a fog, scaring crows. He shouts and waves a rattle. As the day goes on his voice gets weaker till he is hoarse and shouting in a whisper. It gets dark.*
> Scene 1
> *It gets lighter, but still some mist. It is the present.*
> JAPANESE BUSINESSMAN, *in suit, with camera.*
>
> JAPANESE BUSINESSMAN   Mr Takai, Tokyo Company, welcomes you to the fen. Most expensive earth in England. Two thousand pounds acre. Long time ago, under water. Fishes and eels swimming here. Not true people had webbed feet but did walk on stilts ... This farm, one of our twenty-five farms, very good investment. Belongs to Baxter Nolesford Ltd, which belongs to Reindorp Smith Farm Land Trust which belongs 65% to our company ... How beautiful English countryside. I think it is too foggy to take pictures. Now I find teashop, warm fire, old countryman to tell tales.'

Caryl Churchill's opening is deliberately unsettling. How is the play to develop the contrast between the boy and the Japanese businessman? How indeed are the audience to take him? An exploiter or a caricature? No sense of familiar genre guides the audience to secure judgement.

Just as Caryl Churchill refuses to allow a simple response at the start of *Fen*, so she can surprise and shock by dislocation of genre later in the play. Val, a 30-year-old mother, has lost custody of her children to her husband after an affair with Frank; their love is doomed and she thinks of killing herself, but cannot do it. She marks a place with a biro where he is to stick the knife in:

	Val *gives* Frank *the knife*
FRANK	We don't have to do this.
	Silence.
VAL	Say you love me.
FRANK	You know that.
VAL	But say it.
FRANK	I nearly did it. I nearly killed you.
	He puts the knife down.
VAL	Do it. Do it.
FRANK	How can I?
VAL	Just do it
	Silence
FRANK	Aren't you cold? I'm shivering. Let's have a fire and some tea. Eh, Val?
	Frank *picks up an axe and is about to go out.*
	Remember –
VAL	What?
FRANK	Early on. It wasn't going to be like this.
	Silence
	Why do you?
VAL	What?
FRANK	All right then. All right.
	He kills her with the axe.
	He puts her body in the wardrobe.
	He sits on the floor with his back against the wardrobe door.
	She comes in through the door on the other side of the stage.
VAL	It's dark. I can see through you. No, you're better now.
FRANK	Does it go on?
VAL	There's so much happening. There's all those people and I know about them. There's a girl who died. I saw you put me in the wardrobe. I was up by the ceiling. I watched. I could have gone but I wanted to stay with you and I found myself coming back in.

► Analyse this scene, noting the points where it surprises and shocks by changing direction.

The scene starts with a hopelessness that borders on **black comedy**. It then seems about to resolve itself into the domestic normality of a cup of tea, before it snaps into horrific violence. Finally, this shock effect is capped by the melodrama of Val's reappearance as a ghost.

The audience is thus taken by surprise by a play that seems to change its nature and to demand a different kind of response from the one initially signalled. This technique is characteristic of many of the plays of post-war British drama. Sometimes called the 'subversion of genre', it shocks and surprises an audience who are denied the usual reassurance of predictability, and who have to decide for themselves the tone and nature of the play.

Hence an element of uncertainty, of unsettling the audience, is often an important and distinctive feature of British post-war drama. There is sometimes no clear sense of genre; sometimes the play switches from one genre to another, demanding an uncertain or critical response from the audience. This may be true of a whole play: for example, Caryl Churchill's *Top Girls* switches from its opening celebratory party with its fantasy of the modern hostess inviting famous women of the past to a drunken dinner, to the story of her unacknowledged daughter and a broken and dysfunctional relationship. It is left to the audience to relate the two parts of the heroine's life and to come to a conclusion about the play's purpose and meaning. The subversion may occur in a scene – or even within a scene – when the genre and mood changes disturbingly, as has been seen in the extract from *Fen*.

The language of the play

In the beginning is the word. Most plays are scripted and the words form the basis of the drama. The dramatist creates dialogue and speeches, and must decide on an register of speech that is appropriate for the kind of play he or she is writing. A naturalistic play will clearly demand a different kind of language to that appropriate for **poetic drama**.

In the first half of the century, in the dramas of Shaw, Coward and Rattigan, articulacy was expected of all the characters. In Shaw's work discussion was central: the speakers had to show verbal polish and be extremely articulate. Few dustmen could speak in the witty debating tones of Doolittle in *Pygmalion* about the disadvantages of receiving a large annuity:

> 'I, as one of the deserving poor, have nothing between me and this pauper's uniform but this here blasted three thousand a year that thrusts me into the middle class. (Excuse the expression, maam; youd use it yourself if you had my provocation.) They've got you every way you turn: it's a choice between the Skilly of the workhouse and the Char Bydis of the middle class; and I havnt the nerve for the workhouse. Intimidated thats what I am ...'

Shaw wanted his audience to respond to *ideas* about the deserving poor, not to present them on stage to his middle class audience.

When, however, the theatre opened itself up to a wider audience after *Look Back in Anger* in 1956, and with the arrival of inarticulate speakers in the plays of Pinter, Wesker, Bond and Arden, the problem became that of finding an effective dramatic language for them. The answer was not the equivalent of bringing a tape recording onto the stage. All transcriptions of actual speech show how formless and repetitive that can be. The following extract shows how Harold Pinter faced the problem. It is the beginning of Pinter's *The Birthday Party*. Petey returns to the living room of a seaside boarding house. Meg is behind the kitchen hatch:

MEG	Is that you, Petey?
	Pause
	Petey, is that you?
	Pause
	Petey?
PETEY	What?
MEG	Is that you?
PETEY	Yes, it's me.
MEG	What? *[Her face appears at the hatch.]* Are you back?
MEG	I've got your cornflakes ready. *[She disappears and reappears.]* Here's your cornflakes.
	He rises and takes the plate from her, sits at the table, props up the paper and begins to eat. MEG *enters by the kitchen door.*
	Are they nice?
PETEY	Very nice.
MEG	I thought they'd be nice. *[She sits at the table.]* You got your paper?
PETEY	Yes.
MEG	Is it good?
PETEY	Not bad.
MEG	What does it say?
PETEY	Nothing much.
MEG	You read me out some nice bits yesterday.
PETEY	Yes, well, I haven't finished this one yet.
MEG	Will you tell me when you come to something good?
PETEY	Yes.
	Pause.

▶ How close is this to the language of real speech? Look in detail at the extract: where and how has the text been shaped?

One feature that you may have noted is the use of pauses and silence. In a speech given in 1962, Pinter analysed the nature of conversation: 'The speech we hear is an indication of that we don't hear. It is a necessary avoidance, a violent, sly, mocking smokescreen which keeps the other in its place.' So what the audience hears is often misleading, and they have to judge the real 'meaning' beneath the surface of the text. What is *really* being said, as opposed to what the words say, is called the sub-text. It is important to note that Pinter did not invent the idea of the sub-text: it is always invoked when an audience asks: What does this or that character *actually* mean? The presence of the sub-text is crucial not only to Pinter, but also to other playwrights who want to suggest deeper motivations and depths of character, or to show that words are just as likely to conceal as to reveal thoughts.

▶ Write out the sub-text of the extract above to show what you think is the nature of the 'real' conversation.

Dramatic language

The words on the page are not the only way (and some critics would say not even the main way) that a dramatist has to convey his or her meaning. The term 'dramatic language' includes all the physical and visual properties of a play, the use of setting, sound, costume, the stage itself – and how all these mesh together to produce meaning. In the following extract from David Hare's *Plenty* (1978), Susan has recently met a young diplomat, Brock, who has fallen in love with her. Alice is her friend who works with unmarried mothers:

> *Pimlico. September 1947.*
> *From the dark the sound of a string quartet. It comes to an end. Then a voice.*

ANNOUNCER This is the BBC Third Programme. Vorichef wrote *Les Ossifies* in the year of the Paris Commune, but his struggle with Parkinson's disease during the writing of the score has hitherto made it a peculiarly difficult manuscript for musicologists to interpret. However the leader of the Bremen Ensemble has recently done a magnificent work of reclamation. Vorichef died in an extreme state of senile dementia in 1878. This performance of his last work will be followed by a short talk in our series 'Musicians and Disease'.
> *A bed-sitter with some wooden chairs, a bed and a canvas bed with a suitcase set beside it. A small room, well maintained but cheerless.* ALICE *sits on the floor in a*

	chalk-striped men's suit and a white tie. She smokes a
	hookah. SUSAN *is on the edge of the bed drinking cocoa.*
	She is wearing a blue striped shirt. Her revolver lies
	beside her. BROCK *is laid out fast asleep across two*
	chairs in his pinstripes. Next to him is a large pink
	parcel, an odd item of luxury in the dismal
	surroundings. By the way they talk you know it's late.
SUSAN	I want to move on. I do desperately want to feel I'm
	moving on.
ALICE	With him?
SUSAN	Well that's the problem, isn't it?
	Pause. ALICE *smiles.*
ALICE	You are strange.
SUSAN	Well, what would you do?
ALICE	I'd trade him in.

In this passage every detail makes an impact. Pimlico is a contrast to the opulence of Knightsbridge where the play's opening is set. Hare uses darkness to simulate the power of the radio and the string quartet. The bed-sitter itself, with its sparse furnishings, is an image of the rootlessness of its tenant, Susan. Both Alice and Susan are wearing men's clothes, which links them and lends a sexual ambiguity to their relationship. The revolver stands out as a pregnant sign of Susan's fragile self-control. Brock's luxury parcel is an indication of his relationship with Susan, and both the present and his official pinstripes seem out of place in Susan's world. This is confirmed by the dialogue that discusses Brock as an encumbrance, to be traded in like a second-hand car.

▶ Choose one of the play extracts in Part 3 and analyse carefully its dramatic language. Now apply these techniques to a specific scene from one of the plays that you are studying.

Characterisation

Since the time of Aristotle (4th century BC) the response of an audience to character has been seen as a key element in the drama. Drama has always provided a rich store of characters and for many audiences that personal engagement is the necessary condition of successful, interesting drama. This remains at least partly true: the comedies of Alan Ayckbourn, for example, attest to the power of this appeal.

However, the influence of Brecht's so-called 'alienation technique' has modified many dramatists' approach to character. Brecht and those British dramatists who were influenced by him and who adapted his ideas on epic theatre (Bond, Edgar,

Brenton, Hare and many other playwrights of the 1970s) were highly suspicious of the involvement of an audience with a fictional character. They felt it was a kind of bourgeois self-indulgence which distracted from the political and moral importance of a theatre that should change behaviour, not encourage an audience to weep vicarious tears. Hence they developed a kind of theatre (agit-prop) that created caricature rather than character, and a wide canvas of epic theatre that showed the breadth of a society rather than dwelling on the depth of individuality. Dramatists like Hare and Edgar later moved away from the simplicity of agit-prop to develop more complex characters.

As Brecht and those he influenced have found, character is hard to dispense with on the stage. It is important to note that in drama, character is rarely an end in itself. It is through our involvement and interest in character that the themes and preoccupations of the playwright emerge. Through the character of Jimmy Porter, for example, in *Look Back in Anger*, John Osborne deals with his themes of disillusion in post-war Britain. Modern British drama presents a whole spectrum of response to characterisation from little or no interest (for example, satire or agit-prop), to some interest (for example, social realism), to major importance (for example, the psychological thriller, tragedy).

The critic and playwright April de Angelis asks questions about characterisation that may seem appropriate to the 21st century:

> I wonder if we're still entitled to write the kind of characters that have an inside that struggles with the outside and where eventually this struggle brings out some kind of truth.
>
> When I start thinking about plays, I suppose I always accept that notion of character, but there's always a part of me that doesn't really believe it. I really want to believe we have a history, I want to believe we have an inside that's us and that will eventually come out, a truth that is the sum of us and what's happened to us in our histories that will emerge and reveal who we are. But even as I write it, I don't believe it …
>
> This was really brought home to me when I saw Martin Crimp's *Attempts on her Life* upstairs at the Royal Court. I went there and sat and watched and I felt this incredible sense of relief. I thought, 'Thank God, there aren't any people in this play!' It felt so incredibly refreshing. But it also felt really terrifying: if they aren't people, then what on earth are they, and who are we? This play did not define the idea of character … At one point one of the voices in the play believes she's a TV screen, that everything from the front looks real and alive but round the back there's just a few wires. And the playwright believes that we're now in a non-human age, an age of globalisation,

a new multinational capital, an age of surface depthlessness – we're
living in an advert.

(April de Angelis *State of Play* ed. David Edgar, 1999)

▶ According to de Angelis why are traditional attitudes to character inadequate now?
How far do you agree?

▶ The writer and novelist, E.M. Forster, distinguished between 'flat' characters and
'round' characters in fiction. So-called 'flat' characters were two-dimensional and
lacked the ability to surprise. 'Round' characters had real depth and evoked a
response, which was similar to a response to a real friend or partner. Do you find this
a useful distinction in regard to the characters of the plays you have read? Consider
which characters are most 'round' and which are most 'flat'.

The plot's the thing

Aristotle defined drama as 'an imitation of an action'. Classical drama puts a stress
on, and lays down rules for, the construction of plays which should follow certain
familiar patterns. Exposition, complication and resolution were the three basic
elements that made up the form. The well-made play, so popular between the wars,
had a different but no less clear plot structure which led to a 'denouement', literally
an untying of knots, in the last act. The plays of Shaw, J.B. Priestley and Alan
Ayckbourn often follow the template of the well-made play.

Plot in most modern British drama, however, is not nearly so predictable or rule-
bound. Just as dramatists experiment with the notion of genre, so they do with plot.
Indeed, inventiveness and experimentation with plots are a key feature of modern
British drama. In David Hare's *Plenty*, for example, the action begins in 1962,
switches back in time to 1943 and then proceeds chronologically to 1962. The final
scene reverts to wartime France in 1944. In Tom Stoppard's *The Real Thing* (1982),
the first scene presents the drama of a husband discovering his wife's infidelity. In
the second scene, it becomes apparent that the first scene was an excerpt from a
play and the audience has been hoodwinked into asking questions about the nature
of stage reality. In absurdist drama plot may be pared down to the bare minimum, as
in the plays of Samuel Beckett; or fail to offer any clear resolution, as in Harold
Pinter's *The Birthday Party*; or underline the mad logic of the world, as in Joe
Orton's *What The Butler Saw*.

Some feminist critics believe that the dramatic structure that has been a
backbone of the plots of Western drama, the idea of a conflict that builds up through
complication to a climax, is a distinctively masculine idea. This structure has been
subverted by more feminist ideas of dramatic form, for example in the work of Caryl
Churchill. Using examples from her plays, these techniques might include:

- the use of song in *Vinegar Tom* that moves the play from its historical time to the present
- the disruption of the chronological narrative by time switches, as in *Top Girls*
- the use of repetitive scenes, as in *Blue Heart* (1997), in which each repetition marks the inner thought process of a character.

Churchill makes clear by all these devices that she is more interested in examining and questioning than following a conventional narrative plot.

▶ Analyse the plots of the plays that you have read scene by scene. Do they employ a linear narrative? What parallels and/or contrasts does the playwright make? Are there any surprising dislocations of the time scheme, effective contrasts or surprises? If so, why?

Theatre movements

It is helpful to place the plays that are studied within the context of the main forms of dramatic expression, as outlined below.

Realism and epic realism

Realism is a slippery and difficult term and overlaps with naturalism. Characteristic of realism is the use of lifelike settings and dialogue, and a plot which avoids the far-fetched or the romantic. It is different from naturalism in that it focuses less on the trappings of daily life, and more on the issues and conflicts which underlie it.

The playwright David Edgar has described epic realism as the dominant form of the late 1960s, through the 1970s and 1980s. This theatre is political in nature, taking on public themes, often wide-ranging in its subject matter and its time-scale. It relies less on character and more on the exploration of ideas. Edgar's own play *Maydays* (1983) and Howard Brenton's *The Churchill Play* (1974) are good examples of epic realism.

Naturalism and kitchen sink drama

Naturalism attempts to mirror the circumstances of ordinary life. It therefore tends to stress the role of environment in the shaping of events and characters. In one form or another, it is the major mode of drama in the 20th century. The plays of D.H. Lawrence are early examples of naturalism, as are Arnold Wesker's *Roots* (1959) and *Chips with Everything* (1962). Kitchen sink drama is a specific kind of naturalism that focuses on the domestic issues of working class life. This linkage points to the association that naturalism has with the depiction of working class life, but in the sense of 'true to life' it can have a wider application. Television has become the true home of naturalism.

Theatre of the absurd

Theatre of the absurd is a term coined by the critic Martin Esslin in his book of the same name (1962) to link the dramas of Samuel Beckett to those of Pinter and his contemporaries. The absurd encompasses a wide range of dramatic practice. It is in many ways the exact opposite to epic theatre. It tends to stress the individual rather than society, and is based on the unpredictability, oddness or incomprehensibility of the world. In British drama, it has often taken the form of black comedy which is at once funny and disturbing. Joe Orton's *Loot* (1965), Harold Pinter's *The Room* (1960), Steven Berkoff's *Metamorphosis* (1969) and Tom Stoppard's comedies all show the influence and variety of the absurd.

▶ Research these critical terms to give a fuller description of the movements outlined above. (The texts listed under Further reading, pages 119–120, will give you some leads.)

Assignments

1 Compare and contrast in detail the language of any three extracts. You might examine: the articulacy of characters' speech; the sentence structure (long or short, complex or simple?); the vocabulary and imagery (plain or poetic?); the use of sub-text, climaxes, pauses or repetitions. How does the language create character and dramatic effect?

2 How important is character in the plays that you have read?

3 Compare the way that plots are constructed in any two plays you have examined.

4 In what ways does a sense of theatre movement and genre help to illuminate the texts you are reading? Remember that the aim is not to put a play in a particular category, but rather to see how the playwright has used the genre to express his or her purpose.

3 | Play extracts

The extracts that follow have been chosen to illustrate key themes and points made elsewhere in the book, and to provide material which may be useful when working on the tasks and assignments. The items are arranged chronologically.

Stanley Houghton

From *Hindle Wakes* (1912)

Hindle Wakes was first presented by Miss Horniman's Repertory Company from Manchester at the Aldwych Theatre, London in 1912. Fanny Hawthorn, a lively and intelligent mill girl, has deceived her parents and spent an illicit weekend in Llandudno with her boyfriend, Alan Jeffcote, the son of a rich mill-owning family. Alan's fiancée, Beatrice, has rejected him because she feels he is now morally bound to marry Fanny. When both families agree that their children should get married Fanny remains silent, and Alan asks them to withdraw so that he can speak to Fanny alone.

ALAN	But just look here. I'm going to fall between two stools. It's all up with Beatrice, of course. And if you won't have me I shall have parted from her to no purpose; besides getting kicked out of the house by my father, more than likely.
FANNY	Nay, nay! He'll not punish you for this. He doesn't know it's your fault I'm not willing to wed you.
ALAN	He may. It's not fair, but it would be father all over to do that.
FANNY	He'll be only too pleased to get shut of me without eating his own words. He'll forgive you on the spot, and you can make it up with Beatrice tomorrow.
ALAN	I can never make it up with Bee!
FANNY	Get away!
ALAN	You won't understand a girl like Bee. I couldn't think of even trying for months, and then it may be too late. I'm not the only pebble on the beach. And I'm a damaged one, at that!
FANNY	She's fond of you, you said?
ALAN	Yes. I think she's very fond of me.
FANNY	Then she'll make it up in a fortnight.
ALAN	*[moodily]* You said *you* were fond of me once, but it hasn't taken you long to alter.

FANNY	All women aren't built alike. Beatrice is religious. She'll be sorry for you. I was fond of you in a way.
ALAN	But you didn't ever really love me?
FANNY	Love you? Good heavens, of course not. Why on earth should I love you? You were just someone to have a bit of fun with. You were an amusement – a lark.
ALAN	[shocked] Fanny! Is that all you cared for me?
FANNY	How much more did you care for me?
ALAN	But it's not the same. I'm a man.
FANNY	You're a man and I was your little fancy. Well, I'm a woman and *you* were *my* little fancy. You wouldn't prevent a woman enjoying herself as well as a man, if she takes it into her head?
ALAN	But do you mean to say that you didn't care any more for me than a fellow cares for a girl he happens to pick up?
FANNY	Yes. Are you shocked?
ALAN	It's a bit thick; it is really!
FANNY	You're a beauty to talk!
ALAN	It sounds so jolly immoral. I never thought of a girl looking on a chap just like that! I made sure you wanted to marry me if you got the chance.
FANNY	No fear! You're not good enough for me. The chap Fanny Hawthorn weds has got to be made of different stuff from you, my lad. My husband, if ever I have one, will be a man, not a fellow who'll throw over his girl at his father's bidding! Strikes me the sons of these rich manufacturers are all much alike. They seem a bit weak in the upper storey. It's their fathers' brass that's too much for them, happen! They don't know how to spend it properly. They're like chaps who can't carry their drink because they aren't used to it. The brass gets into their heads, like!
ALAN	Hang it, Fanny, I'm not quite a fool.
FANNY	No. You're not a fool altogether. But there's summat lacking. You're not man enough for me. You're a nice lad, and I'm fond of you. But I couldn't ever marry you. We've had a right good time together, I'll never forget that. It *has* been a right good time, and no mistake! We've enjoyed ourselves proper! But all good times have to come to an end, and ours is over now. Come along now, and bid me farewell.
ALAN	I can't make you out rightly, Fanny, but you're a damn

	good sort, and I wish there were more like you!
FANNY	*[holding out her hand]* Good-bye, old lad.
ALAN	*[grasping her hand]* Good-bye, Fanny! And good luck!

Harold Brighouse

From *Hobson's Choice* (1916)

Harold Brighouse was a friend of Stanley Houghton and together they were the leading playwrights of 'The Manchester School', based on the Gaiety Theatre in Manchester.

Brighouse wrote his comedy of Victorian Salford, where he was born, in 1914, but it was initially considered too serious for wartime entertainment in Britain. It therefore received its first performance in New York in 1915 and in London in 1916. Henry Horatio Hobson is a self-made Victorian cobbler and shopkeeper who employs the timidly talented William Mossop. Hobson's strong-minded daughter, Maggie, marries Willie and helps him to transform his weakness of character. The extract is the end of the play.

WILLIE	*[opening door and looking through]* I'll make some alterations in this shop, and all. I will so. *[He goes through door and returns at once with a battered cane chair.]*
HOBSON	Alterations in my shop!
WILLIE	In mine. Look at that chair. How can you expect the high-class customers to come and sit on a chair like that? Why, we'd only a cellar, but they did sit on cretonne for their trying on.
DOBSON	Cretonne! It's pampering folk.
WILLIE	Cretonne for a cellar and morocco for this shop. Folk like to be pampered. Pampering pays. *[He takes the chair out and returns immediately.]* There'll be a carpet on that floor, too.
HOBSON	Carpet! Morocco! Young man, do you think this shop is in Saint Ann's Square, Manchester?
WILLIE	Not yet. But it's going to be.
HOBSON	What does he mean? *[Appealing to heaven.]*
WILLIE	It's no farther from Chapel Street to Saint Ann's Square than it is from Oldfield Road to Chapel Street. I've done one jump in a year and if I wait a bit I'll do the other. Maggie, I reckon your father could do with a bit of fresh air after this. ... Suppose you walk with him to Albert

	Prosser's office and get Albert to draw up the deed of partnership.
HOBSON	*[looking pathetically first at* MAGGIE, *then at* WILLIE, *rising obediently]* I'll go and get my hat.
	Exit HOBSON
WILLIE	He's crushed-like, Maggie. I'm afraid I bore on him too hard.
MAGGIE	You needn't be.
WILLIE	I said such things to him, and they sounded as if I meant them, too.
MAGGIE	Didn't you?
WILLIE	Did I? Yes … I suppose I did. That's just the worst … from me to him. You told me to be strong and to use the power that's come to me through you, but he's the old master, and –
MAGGIE	And you're the new.
WILLIE	Master of Hobson's! It's an outrageous big idea. Did I sound confident, Maggie?
MAGGIE	You did all right.
WILLIE	Eh, but I weren't by half so certain as I sounded. Words came from my mouth that made me jump at my own boldness, and when it came to facing you about the name, I tell you I fair trembled in my shoes. I was carried away like, or I'd not have dared to cross you, Maggie.
MAGGIE	Don't spoil it, Will. *[Moves to him.]* You're the man I've made you and I'm proud.
WILLIE	Thy pride is not in same street, lass, with the pride I have in you. And that reminds me. I've a job to see to.
MAGGIE	What job?
WILLIE	Oh – about the improvements.
MAGGIE	You'll not do owt without consulting me.
WILLIE	I'll do this, lass. *[Goes to and takes her hand.]*
MAGGIE	Where are you going? You leave my wedding ring alone. *[Wrenches hand free.]*
WILLIE	You've worn a brass one long enough.
MAGGIE	I'll wear that ring for ever, Will.
WILLIE	I was for getting you a proper one, Maggie.
MAGGIE	I'm not preventing you. I'll wear your gold for show, but that brass stays where you put it, Will, and if we get too rich and proud we'll just sit down together quiet and take a long look at it, so as we'll not forget the truth about ourselves … Eh, lad! *[She touches him affectionately.]*

WILLIE	Eh, lass! *[He kisses her.]*
	Enter HOBSON *with his hat on.*
MAGGIE	Ready, father. Come along to Albert's.
HOBSON	*[meekly]* Yes, Maggie.
	MAGGIE *and* HOBSON *cross below* WILLIE *and go out.* WILLIE *comes down with amazement, triumph and incredulity written on his face, and attempts to express the inexpressible by saying –*
WILLIE	Well, by gum! *[He turns to follow the others.]*

Tom Thomas

From *Their Theatre and Ours* (1932)

This extract illustrates many of the features of agit-prop. Tom Thomas notes 'it is vital that the strongest contrast in style be made between the burlesque inset scenes of the capitalist theatre and films, and the serious passages'. The extract follows the opening of the piece when 'The troupe marches on, well-disciplined, singing enthusiastically and in well-marked rhythm' a rousing song with the refrain 'We're Worker Players, Red Worker Players …'

ALL	WORKERS' THEATRE! WORKERS' THEATRE! WORKERS' THEATRE!
1ST	The theatre of workers like yourselves
2ND	Who play in every town and country
3RD	To workers like yourselves
ALL	WORKERS' THEATRE! WORKERS' THEATRE! WORKERS THEATRE!
4TH	We show the life of working men and women
5TH	Their hardships and their hunger
6TH	Their struggles to exist
1ST	We are robbed at work for the profits of the rich!
2ND	They speed us up, and throw millions out of work!
3RD	Three millions of us and more are out of work!
4TH	They cut the dole and put us on the Means Test
5TH	But the landlord gets his rent, or throws us out on the ear.
6TH	The bondholders get their hundreds of millions in interest every year.
WOMAN PLAYER	Workers' children are robbed of their milk
ANOTHER WOMAN	And the death rate of the workers' children rises.
3RD	*[to audience]* Why don't we workers unite and end

	this misery, this starvation, this mass-murder?
1ST	*Because* many workers are still satisfied with their rotten conditions.
2ND	*Because* others think that the workers have always been poor and oppressed and always *will* be.
4TH	*Because* thousands more think that the rich class are too powerful for us to overthrow.
5TH	And why do they think like this?
6TH	*Because* the capitalist class make you think just exactly what they want you to think.
1ST	The press
2ND	The schools
3RD	The theatres
4TH	The cinemas
ALL	Are controlled by the capitalist class.
2ND	When things get bad, they sing to you at the pictures –
	[The group gather round like a chorus on stage or film 'plugging' a 'cheer-up' song. A satirical picture of the way this stuff is put across. Faces ghastly with forced happiness. 2ND leads them in the song.]
	'Happy days here again, The skies above are clear again'. *[Straight on to]* 'There's a good time coming. So keep your sunny side up, up' –
	[All break off singing suddenly and become a worker audience coming out of a show.]
1ST	*[enthusiastic]* Good show, that!
3RD	*[wearily]* Not bad.
1ST	Nice and cheerful!
3RD	It's about the only thing that is!
4TH	Don't I know it? I've been out nearly four years. Just lost one of my little ones – couldn't feed her properly.
5TH	And we're all working short time – and speeded up like mad while we're there.
6TH	Yes, and by the time you've paid the landlord and the clubs there's nothing left to live on.
4TH	What we want is a revolution!
1ST	*[still cheerful]* Cheer up, mate. There's a good time coming!
3RD	*[laughing sourly]* So keep your sunny side up – eh?
1ST	*[sings softly to himself]* Sing Hallelujah, Hallelujah and you'll shoo your blues away.
2ND	*[breaks into scene; the others go off quickly]* And

	that's how they do it on you. There's always a good time coming – but the workers never get it.
3RD	And when in 1914 the bosses drove us to fight their bloody war for them, to increase their profits – their theatres and cinemas did the dirty work
GIRL	[enters and sings to audience in heavily emphasised music-hall style] For we don't want to lose you, but we think you ought to go, for your king and your country both need you so.
ANOTHER GIRL	And one million men who were caught like this never came back but died ghastly tortured deaths for the profits of the capitalist class.
MAN	And thousands who did come back are tramping the streets – unemployed – unwanted – outcasts – And what do the king and the country care?

John Osborne

From *Look Back in Anger* (1956)

John Osborne's play has been claimed as the turning point of British drama in the second half of the 20th century. When it appeared in 1956 many reviews were lukewarm or hostile, but after an ecstatic review from Kenneth Tynan and a television broadcast it came to be seen as a groundbreaking moment. Jimmy Porter is a working-class university graduate who has married the upper-middle class Alison. In this scene, set in their one-room flat, Jimmy is attacking his wife with his usual relish. Cliff is an old friend.

JIMMY	Have you ever seen her brother? Brother Nigel? The straight-backed chinless wonder from Sandhurst? I only met him once myself. He asked me to step outside when I told his mother she was evil minded.
CLIFF	And did you?
JIMMY	Certainly not. He's a big chap. Well, you've never heard so many well-bred commonplaces come from beneath the same bowler hat. The Platitude from Outer Space – that's brother Nigel. He'll end up in the Cabinet one day, make no mistake. But somewhere at the back of that mind is the vague knowledge that he and his pals have been plundering and fooling everybody for generations. [Going upstage and turning.] Now Nigel is just about as vague as you can get without being actually invisible.

And invisible politicians aren't much use to anyone – not even to *his* supporters! And nothing is more vague about Nigel than his knowledge. His knowledge of life and ordinary human beings is so hazy, he really deserves some sort of decoration for it – a medal inscribed 'For Vaguery in the Field'. But it wouldn't do for him to be troubled by any stabs of conscience, however vague. *[Moving down again.]* Besides he's a patriot and an Englishman, and he doesn't like the idea that he may have been selling out his countryman all these years, so what does he do? The only thing he *can* do – seek sanctuary in his own stupidity. The only way to keep things as much like they always have been as possible, is to make any alternative too much for your poor, tiny brain to grasp. It takes some doing nowadays. It really does. But they knew all about character building at Nigel's school, and he'll make it all right. Don't you worry, he'll make it. And, what's more, he'll do it better than anybody else!

There is no sound, only the plod of Alison's iron. Her eyes are fixed on what she is doing. Cliff stares at the floor. His cheerfulness has deserted him for the moment. Jimmy is rather shakily triumphant. He cannot allow himself to look at either of them to catch their response to his rhetoric, so he moves across to the window, to recover himself, and look out.

It's started to rain. That's all it needs. This room and the rain.

He's been cheated out of his response, but he's got to draw blood somehow.

[conversationally) Yes, that's the little woman's family. You know Mummy and Daddy, of course. And don't let the Marquess of Queensbury manner fool you. They'll kick you in the groin while you're handing your hat to the maid.

Arnold Wesker

From *Roots* (1960)

Roots was the second part of a trilogy dealing with the Kahn family. In this extract, taken from the end of the play, Beatie Bryant, the daughter of Norfolk farmworkers, has had a relationship with Ronnie, the son of an intellectual Jewish working class family. After he has rejected her, she feels that she has little in common with her family but, equally, that she does not belong in Ronnie's world. She argues that the problem with her family is that their apathy prevents them from living life to the full

MRS BRYANT	Blust woman – bored you say, bored? You say Susie's bored, with a radio and television an that? ...
BEATIE	Oh yes, we turn on a radio or a TV set maybe, or we go to the pictures – if them's love stories or gangsters – but isn't that the easiest way out? Anything so long as we don't have to make an effort. Well, am I right? You know I'm right. Education ent only books and music – it's asking questions, all the time. There are millions of us, all over the country, and no one, not one of us, is asking questions, we're all taking the easiest way out. ... We don't fight for anything, we're so mentally lazy we might as well be dead. Blust, we are dead! And you know what Ronnie says sometimes? He say it serves us right! That's what he say – it's our own bloody fault!
JIMMY	So that's us summed up then – so we know where *we* are then!
MRS BRYANT	Well if he don't reckon we count nor nothin', then it's as well he didn't come.
BEATIE	Oh, *he* thinks we count all right – living in mystic communion with nature. Living in mystic bloody communion with nature (indeed). But us count? Count Mother? I wonder. Do we? Do you think we really count? You don' wanna take any notice of what them ole papers say about the workers bein' all-important these days – that's all squit! 'Cos we aren't. Do you think when the really talented people in the country get to work they get to work for us? Hell if they do! Do you think they don't know we 'ont make the effort? The writers don't write thinkin' we can understand, nor the painters don't paint expecting us to be interested – that they don't, nor don't the composers give out music thinking we can appreciate it. 'Blust,' they say, 'the masses is too stupid for us to come down to them. Blust,' they say, 'if they don't make no effort why should we bother?' So you know who come along? The slop singers and the pop writers and the film makers and the picture strip love stories – that's who come

along, and you don't have to make no effort for them, it come easy. 'We know where the money lie,' they say, 'hell we do! The workers've got it so let's give them what they want. If they want slop songs and film idols we'll give 'em that then. If they want words of one syllable, we'll give 'em that then. ... If they want third-rate, *blust*! We'll give 'em that then. Anything's good enough for them 'cos they don't ask for no more!' The whole stinkin' commercial world insults us and we don't care a damn. Well, Ronnie's right – it's our own bloody fault. We want the third-rate – we got it! We got it! We got it! We ...

[*Suddenly* BEATIE *stops as if listening to herself. She pauses, turns with an ecstatic smile on her face –]*

D'you hear that? D'you hear it? Did you listen to me? I'm talking, Jenny, Frankie, Mother – I'm not quoting no more.

MRS BRYANT   [*getting up to sit at table*] Oh hell, I hed enough of her – let her talk awhile she'll soon get fed up.

[*The others join her at the table and proceed to eat and murmur.*]

BEATIE   Listen to me someone. [*As though a vision were revealed to her*] God in Heaven, *Ronnie!* It does work, it's happening to me, I can feel it's happened, I'm beginning to stand on my own two feet – I'm beginning ...

Theatre Workshop

From *Oh, What a Lovely War!* (1963)

This play was the great West End success of Joan Littlewood's Theatre Workshop. The stage setting is of a *pierrot* show just before the First World War. There is a news panel above the stage on which are projected headlines, war news and statistics. Slides of the war are projected onto a backstage screen. In its mixture of song, dance, newspaper headlines and photographic images, the play is an example of the techniques of **total theatre**.

M.C.   Milords, ladies and gentlemen, may we perform for you the ever-popular War Game!

BAND   MARCH OF THE GLADIATORS
Circus Parade: two pierrot acrobats lead on the

	company dressed in national costumes. A French group of three pierrots – one man (a French army officer), two women; a German group – the Kaiser and a woman, Austria; a British group of five – a woman, Ireland, leading, a British colonial on the shoulders of another, followed by a fan-holder, and a coloured servant; Russian group of two men. The company move round the stage in a circle as in a circus parade, finally stopping, keeping the circular shape ...
NEWSPANEL	TROOPS FIRE ON DUBLIN CROWD – AUG 1 BRITISH CABINET VOTE AGAINST HELPING FRANCE IF WAR COMES – LIBERALS VOTE FOR NEUTRALITY UNDER ANY CIRCUMSTANCES – GERMANY SENDS 40,000 RIFLES TO ULSTER.
M.C.	*[as the nations pass]* La Belle France – Upright, steadfast Germany – Good morning, sir – the first part of the game is called 'Find the Thief'.
BAND	SONS OF THE SEA
BRITAIN	Look here, we own 30 million square miles of colonies. The British Empire is the most magnificent example of working democracy the world has ever seen.
VOICE	Hear absolutely hear.
M.C.	And the lady on my right.
BAND	SI LE VIN EST BON
FRENCHWOMAN	La République.
FRENCHMAN	The seat of reason, the centre of world civilisation – culture and l'amour.
M.C.	They're at it again. Stop it. If they're not doing that they're eating. How big's your acreage?
FRENCHWOMAN	Six million square kilometres.
M.C.	And you?
BAND	GERMAN MUSIC
KAISER	Germany – a mere three million square kilometres. But we are a new nation united only since 1871.
FRENCHMAN	When you stole Alsace-Lorraine.
KAISER	Ours, German.
M.C.	Hey, we haven't started to play the game yet.
KAISER	We are a disciplined, moral, industrious people. We want more say in the world's affairs.
M.C.	Have to keep an eye on you ... *[to the band]* Let's have the Russian anthem. You're in the three-mile limit. You're all right.
BAND	RUSSIAN ANTHEM

RUSSIA	They're all Yids.
NEWSPANEL	CHURCHILL SENDS FLEET TO SCAPA FLOW.

Harold Pinter

From *The Homecoming* (1965)

This extract is the end of the play. Max, a man of 70, has three sons. The eldest, Teddy, an American academic, has brought his wife, Ruth, home on a visit. The family has decided that she will work as a kept prostitute and live with them. Teddy has returned to America. Sam, Max's brother, has apparently died of a heart attack.

	MAX *turns to* LENNY.
MAX	I'm too old, I suppose. She thinks I'm an old man.
	Pause
	I'm not such an old man.
	Pause
	[To RUTH*]*
	You think I'm too old for you?
	Pause
	Listen. You think you're just going to get that big slag all the time? You think you're just going to have him … you're going to just have him all the time? You're going to have to work! You'll have to take them on, you understand?
	Pause
	Does she realise that?
	Pause
	Lenny, do you think she understands …
	He begins to stammer
	Wait … what … what … we're getting at? What … we've got in mind? Do you think she's got it clear?
	Pause
	I don't think she's got it clear.
	Pause
	You understand what I mean? Listen, I've got a funny idea she'll do the dirty on us, you want to bet? She'll use us, she'll make use of us, I can tell you! I can smell it! You want to bet?
	Pause
	She won't … be adaptable!
	He begins to groan, clutches his stick, falls on to his

*knees by the side of her chair. His body sags. The
groaning stops. His body straightens. He looks at her,
still kneeling.*
I'm not an old man.
Pause
Do you hear me?
He raises his face to her.
Kiss me.
She continues to touch JOEY'S *head, lightly.*
LENNY *stands, watching.*
Curtain

Edward Bond

From *Saved* (1965)

Edward Bond's *Saved* was notorious for the centrepiece scene in which a baby in a pram was stoned to death by a group of young men. The scene and the play aroused such strong reactions that fights broke out in the interval of the first performance and at its American premiere. Bond was pleased to note the large number of the audience who walked out.

The scene is set in a park on a summer afternoon. Fred has been fishing when his girlfriend Pam, whom he now wants to discard, comes in with a pram containing their child. The child has been drugged with aspirins to keep it quiet. This extract is the culmination of a series of incidents: firstly, the pram has been pushed around viciously between the men, then they punch, spit on, then hit the baby. Largely as a result of this scene, the play was banned, and received its first public British performance after the abolition of censorship in 1968.

	PETE *throws a stone to* FRED. FRED *doesn't try to catch it.* *It falls on the ground.* COLIN *picks it up and gives it to* FRED.
MIKE	*[quietly]* Reckon it's all right?
COLIN	*[quietly]* No one around.
PETE	*[quietly]* They don't know it's us.
MIKE	*[quietly]* She left it.
BARRY	It's done now.
PETE	*[quietly]* Yer can do what yer like.
BARRY	Might as well enjoy ourselves.
PETE	*[quietly]* You don't get a chance like this everyday. FRED *throws the stone.*

COLIN	Missed.
PETE	That ain't.
	He throws a stone.
BARRY	Or that!
	He throws a stone.
MIKE	Yeh.
COLIN	*[running round]* Where's all the stones?
MIKE	*[also running round]* Stick it up the fair!
PETE	Liven 'Ampstead 'eath. Three throws a quid! Make a packet. ...
COLIN	*[throws a stone]* Right in the lug 'ole.
	FRED looks for a stone.
PETE	Get its 'ooter.
BARRY	An' its slasher!
FRED	*[picks up a stone, spits on it]* For luck, the sod.
	He throws.
BARRY	Yyooowww!
MIKE	'Ear it plonk!
	A bell rings.
MIKE	'Oo's got the matches?
	He finds some in his pocket.
BARRY	What yer doin'?
COLIN	Wan'a buck up!
MIKE	Keep a look out.
	He starts to throw burning matches in the pram. BARRY *throws a stone. It just misses* MIKE.
	Look out yer bleedin' git!
COLIN	Guy Fawkes!
PETE	Bloody nutter! Put that out!
MIKE	No! You 'ad what you want!
PETE	Yer'll 'ave the 'ol' bloody park 'ere!
	A bell rings.
BARRY	Piss on it! Piss on it!
COLIN	Gungy slasher.
MIKE	Call the R.S.P.C.A.
	A bell rings.
FRED	They'll shut the gates.
PETE	*[going]* There's an 'ole in the railin's.
BARRY	'Old on.
	He looks for a stone.
PETE	Leave it!
BARRY	Just this one!
	He throws a stone and PETE *pushes him over. It goes wide.*

	Bastard!
	To PETE. Yer put me off!
PETE	I'll throttle yer!
BARRY	I got to get it once more!
	The others have gone up left. He takes a stone from the pram and throws it at point blank range. Hits.
	Yar!
COLIN	Where's this 'ole?
MIKE	Yer bleedin' gear!
FRED	Chriss.
	He runs down to the rod and boxes. He picks them up.
BARRY	Bleedin' little sod!
	He hacks into the pram. He goes up left.
PETE	Come on!
	A bell rings. FRED *has difficulty with the boxes and rod. He throws a box away.*
FRED	'Ang on!
	He goes up left.
	They go off up left, making a curious buzzing. A long pause. PAM *comes in down left.*
PAM	I might a know'd they'd a left yer. Lucky yer got someone t' look after yer. Muggins 'ere.
	She starts to push the pram. She does not look into it. She speaks in a sing-song voice, loudly but to herself.
	'Oo's 'ad yer balloon. Thass a present from grannie. Goin' a keep me up 'alf the night? Go t' sleepies. Soon be 'ome. Nice an' warm, then. No one else wants yer. Nice an' warm. Soon be 'omies.

Harold Pinter

From *Landscape* (1968)

At the end of Pinter's *Landscape*, first produced on BBC radio in 1968, the two characters sit at opposite sides of a kitchen table in a house that seems to belong to their dead employer. Beth, in her late 40s, never looks at Duff. Neither 'appears to hear the other's voice'.

DUFF

… I thought you would come into my arms and kiss me, even … offer yourself to me. I would have had you in front of the dog, like a man, in the hall, on the stone, banging the gong, mind you don't get the

scissors up your arse, or the thimble, don't worry, I'll throw them for
the dog to chase, the thimble will keep the dog happy, he'll play with
it with his paws, you'll plead with me like a woman, I'll bang the gong
on the floor, if the sound is too flat, lacks resonance, I'll hang it back
on its hook, bang you against it swinging, gonging, waking the place
up, calling them all for dinner, lunch is up, bring out the bacon, bang
your lovely head, mind the dog doesn't swallow the thimble, slam –
Silence

BETH

He lay above me and looked down at me. He supported my shoulder.
Pause
So tender his touch on my neck. So softly his kiss on my cheek.
Pause
My hand on his rib.
Pause
So sweetly the sand over me. Tiny the sand on my skin.
Pause
So silent the sky in my eyes. Gently the sound of the tide.
Pause
Oh my true love I said.

Tom Stoppard

From *The Real Inspector Hound* (1968)

Two critics, Moon and Birdboot, are watching a conventional country house
mystery play. Mrs Drudge is, of course, the servant.

MRS DRUDGE	*[into phone]* Hello, the drawing-room of Lady Muldoon's country residence one morning in early spring? … *Hello!* – the draw— Who? Who did you wish to speak to? I'm afraid there's no one of that name here, this is all very mysterious and I'm sure it's leading up to something. I hope nothing is amiss for we, that is Lady Muldoon and her houseguests, are here cut off from the world, including Magnus, the wheelchair-ridden half-brother of her Ladyship's husband Lord Albert Muldoon who ten years ago went out for a walk on the cliffs and was never seen again – and all alone, for they had no children.
MOON	Derivative, of course.
BIRDBOOT	But quite sound.

MRS DRUDGE   Should a stranger enter our midst, which I very much
doubt, I will tell him you called. Good-bye.
*[She puts down the phone and catches sight of the
previously seen suspicious character who has now
entered again, more suspiciously than ever, through the
french windows. He senses her stare, freezes, and
straightens up.]*

SIMON   Ah! – hello there! I'm Simon Gascoyne, I hope you don't
mind, the door was open so I wandered in. I'm a friend
of Lady Muldoon, the lady of the house, having made
her acquaintance through a mutual friend, Felicity
Cunningham, shortly after moving into this
neighbourhood just the other day.

MRS DRUDGE   I'm Mrs Drudge. I don't live in but I pop in on my bicycle
when the weather allows to help in the running of
charming though somewhat isolated Muldoon Manor.
Judging by the time *[she glances at the clock]* you did
well to get here before high water cut us off for all
practical purposes from the outside world.

SIMON   I took the short cut over the cliffs and followed one of
the old smugglers' paths through the treacherous
swamps that surround this strangely inaccessible
house.

MRS DRUDGE   Yes, many visitors have remarked on the topographical
quirk in the local strata whereby there are no roads
leading from the Manor, though there *are* ways of
getting *to* it, weather allowing.

SIMON   Yes, well I must say it's a lovely day so far.

MRS DRUDGE   Ah, now that the cuckoo-beard is in bud there'll be fog
before the sun hits Foster's Ridge.

Caryl Churchill

From *Top Girls* (1982)

First produced at The Royal Court Theatre, London, *Top Girls* opens with a dinner
party to celebrate the promotion of Marlene, the hostess, to Managing Director of
the 'Top Girls' employment agency. She has invited a group of successful women
from the past. Lady Nijo fled the court of medieval Japan to become an itinerant
Buddhist nun. Isabella Bird was an intrepid Scottish traveller in Victorian times
who, in advanced years, travelled through Tibet and China and, at 70, became the
first European woman to see the Emperor of Morocco. Joan, disguised as a man,

according to legend, became Pope in 854. Dull Gret is the subject of a painting by Breughel in which she is shown as a warrior fighting the devils in Hell. Caryl Churchill uses the / symbol to indicate one character interrupting another, and the * to indicate overlapping speech.

NIJO	There was nothing in my life, nothing, without the Emperor's favour. The Empress had always been my enemy, Marlene, she said I had no right to wear three-layered gowns. / But I was the adopted daughter of my grandfather the Prime Minister. I had been publicly granted permission to wear thin silk.
JOAN	There was nothing in my life except my studies. I was obsessed with pursuit of the truth. I taught at the Greek School in Rome, which St. Augustine had made famous. I was poor, I worked hard. I spoke apparently brilliantly, I was still very young. I was a stranger; suddenly I was quite famous, I was everyone's favourite. Huge crowds came to hear me. The day after they made me cardinal I fell ill and lay two weeks without speaking, full of terror and regret. / But then I got up
MARLENE	Yes, success is very …
JOAN	Determined to go on. I was seized again / with a desperate longing for the absolute.
ISABELLA	Yes, yes, to go on. I sat in Tobermory among Hennie's flowers and sewed a complete outfit in Jaeger flannel. / I was fifty-six years old.
NIJO	Out of favour but I didn't die. I left on foot, nobody saw me go. For the next twenty years I walked through Japan.
GRET	Walking is good.
	The WAITRESS *enters.*
JOAN	Pope Leo died and I was chosen. All right then. I would be Pope. I would know God. I would know everything.
ISABELLA	I determined to leave my grief behind and set off for Tibet.
MARLENE	Magnificent all of you. We need some more wine, please, two bottles I think. Griselda isn't even here yet, and I want to drink a toast to you all.
ISABELLA	To yourself surely, / we're here to celebrate your success.
NIJO	Yes, Marlene.
JOAN	Yes, what is it exactly, Marlene?

MARLENE	Well it's not Pope but it is managing director. *
JOAN	And you find work for people.
MARLENE	Yes, an employment agency.
NIJO	*Over all the women you work with. And the men.
ISABELLA	And very well deserved too. I'm sure it's just the beginning of something extraordinary.
MARLENE	Well it's worth a party.
ISABELLA	To Marlene. *
MARLENE	And all of us.
JOAN	* Marlene.
NIJO	Marlene.
GRET	Marlene.
MARLENE	We've all come a long way. To our courage and the way we changed our lives and our extraordinary achievements.
	They laugh and drink a toast.

Tom Stoppard

From *The Real Thing* (1982)

Henry is a professional dramatist; his partner is Annie. She has asked Henry if he would rewrite a piece of what he regards as an inferior political drama, written by a young soldier called Brodie. Brodie has been imprisoned for a political protest.

HENRY	Cut it and shape it. Henry of Mayfair. Look – he can't write. I would have to write it for him.
ANNIE	Well, write it for him.
HENRY	I can't.
ANNIE	Why?
HENRY	Because it's *balls*. ... announcing every stale revelation of the newly enlightened, like stout Cortez coming upon the Pacific – war is profits, politicians are puppets, Parliament is a farce, justice is a fraud, property is theft ... It's all here: the Stock Exchange, the arms dealers, the press barons ... You can't fool Brodie – patriotism is propaganda, religion is a con trick, royalty is an anachronism ... Pages and pages of it. It's like being run over very slowly by a travelling freak show of favourite simpletons, the india rubber pedagogue, the midget intellectual, the human panacea ...
ANNIE	It's his view of the world. Perhaps from where he's

	standing you'd see it the same way.
HENRY	Or perhaps I'd realise where I'm standing. Or at least that I'm standing *somewhere*. There is, I suppose, a world of objects which have a certain form, like this coffee mug. I turn it and it has no handle. I tilt it, and it has no cavity. But there is something real here which is always a mug with a handle. I suppose. But politics, justice, patriotism – they aren't even like coffee mugs. There's nothing real there separate from our perception of them. So if you try to change them as though there were something to change, you'll get frustrated, and frustration will finally make you violent. If you know this and proceed with humility, you may perhaps alter people's perceptions so that they behave a little differently at that axis of behaviour where we locate politics or justice; but if you don't know this, then you're acting on a mistake. Prejudice is the expression of this mistake.
ANNIE	Or such is your perception.
HENRY	All right.
ANNIE	And who wrote it, why he wrote it, *where* he wrote it – none of these things count with you?
HENRY	Leave me out of it. They don't count. Maybe Brodie got a raw deal, maybe he didn't. I don't know. It doesn't count. He's a lout with language. I can't help somebody who thinks, or thinks he thinks, that editing a newspaper is censorship, or that throwing bricks is a demonstration while building tower blocks is social violence, or that unpalatable statement is provocation while disrupting the speaker is the exercise of free speech … Words don't deserve that kind of malarkey. They're innocent, neutral, precise, standing for this, describing that, meaning the other, so if you look after them you can build bridges across incomprehension and chaos. But when they get their corners knocked off, they're no good any more, and Brodie knocks corners off without knowing he's doing it. So everything he builds is jerry-built. It's rubbish. An intelligent child could push it over. I don't think writers are sacred, but words are. They deserve respect. If you get the right ones in the right order, you can nudge the world a little or make a poem which children will speak for you when you're dead.

	[ANNIE *goes to the typewriter, pulls out the page from the machine and reads it.*]
ANNIE	'Seventy-nine. Interior. Commander's capsule. From Zadok's p.o.v. we see the green glow of the laser strike-force turning towards us. BCU Zadok's grim smile. *Zadok:* "I think it'd going to work. Here they come!" *Kronk*, voice over: "Hold your course!" *Zadok* –'
HENRY	[*interrupts*] That's not words, that's pictures. The movies. Anyway, alimony doesn't count. If Charlotte made it legal with that architect she's shacked up with, I'd be writing the real stuff.

Timberlake Wertenbaker

From *Our Country's Good* (1988)

Our Country's Good is set in Australia in 1789. After a good dinner and plenty of tongue-loosening wine, the officers are discussing the suggestion that the convicts should put on a play to celebrate the king's birthday. The play chosen is a restoration comedy based on a recruiting sergeant called Kite. Captain Arthur Phillip is the Governor of New South Wales and Ralph is a young Second Lieutenant.

PHILLIP	The theatre is an expression of civilisation. We belong to a great country which has spawned great playwrights: Shakespeare, Marlowe, Jonson, and even in our own time, Sheridan. The convicts will be speaking a refined, literate language and expressing sentiments of a delicacy they are not used to. It will remind them that there is more to life than crime, punishment. And we, this colony of a few hundred will be watching this together, for a few hours we will no longer be despised prisoners and hated gaolers. We will laugh, we may be moved, we may even think a little. Can you suggest something else that will provide such an evening, Watkin?
DAWES	Mapping the stars gives me more enjoyment, personally.
TENCH	I'm not sure it's a good idea having the convicts laugh at officers, Arthur.
CAMPBELL	No. Pheeoh, insubordination, heh, ehh, no discipline.
ROSS	You want this vice-ridden vermin to enjoy themselves?

COLLINS	They would only laugh at Sergeant Kite.
RALPH	Captain Plume is a most attractive, noble fellow.
REVD JOHNSON	He's not loose, is he Ralph? I hear many of these plays are about rakes and encourage loose morals in women. They do get married? Before, that is, before. And for the right reasons.
RALPH	They marry for love and to secure wealth.
REVD JOHNSON	That's all right.
TENCH	I would simply say that if you want to build a civilisation there are more important things than a play. If you want to teach the convicts something, teach them to farm, to build houses, teach them a sense of respect for property, teach them thrift so they don't eat a week's rations in one night, but above all, teach them how to work, not how to sit around laughing at a comedy.
PHILLIP	The Greeks believed that it was a citizen's duty to watch plays. It was a kind of work in that it required attention, judgement, patience, all social virtues.
TENCH	And the Greeks were conquered by the more practical Romans, Arthur.
COLLINS	Indeed, the Romans built their bridges, but they also spent many centuries wishing they were Greeks. And they, after all, were conquered by barbarians, or by their own corrupt and small spirits.
TENCH	Are you saying Rome would not have fallen if the theatre had been better?
RALPH	*[very loud]* Why not? *[Everyone looks at him and he continues, fast and nervously.]* In my own small way, in just a few hours, I have seen something change. I asked some of the convict women to read me some lines, these women who behave often no better than animals. And it seemed to me, as one or two – I'm not saying all of them, not at all – but one or two, saying those well-balanced lines of Mr Farquhar, they seemed to acquire a dignity, they seemed – to lose some of their corruption. There was one, Mary Brenham, she read so well, perhaps this play will keep her from selling herself to the first marine who offers her bread –
FADDY	*[under his breath]* She'll sell herself to him instead.
ROSS	So that's the way the wind blows –
CAMPBELL	Hooh. A tempest. Hooh.
RALPH	*[over them]* I speak about her, but in a small way this could affect all the convicts and even ourselves, we

	could forget our worries about the supplies, the hangings and the floggings, and think of ourselves at the theatre, in London with our wives and children, that is, we could, euh –
PHILLIP	Transcend –
RALPH	Transcend the darker, euh – transcend the –
JOHNSON	Brutal –
RALPH	The brutality – remember our better nature and remember –
COLLINS	England.
RALPH	England.

David Hare

From *Amy's View* (1997)

In this extract from David Hare's play, set in rural Berkshire in 1979, Amy has brought her new boyfriend, Dominic, to meet her mother, Esme, an established actress. Dominic, at the age of 22, is a very successful broadcaster, and he wishes to interview Esme for his television programme. Frank is Esme's friend who works in the City.

ESME	Dominic's planning this programme. We all sit under spotlights. In a studio. Debating
FRANK	And what is the subject to be?
	[ESME *looks sweetly at* DOMINIC.]
ESME	No, really. It's your idea. Tell him.
DOMINIC	We're discussing the question of whether the theatre is dead.
	[*There is a slightly sticky moment.*]
AMY	Dead?
FRANK	Oh, I see.
DOMINIC	I told you that, Amy.
AMY	I didn't realise it was quite as dramatic as that.
DOMINIC	Well, we might as well face it. It is a real question. To people of my generation at least. In the old days it seemed like theatre was really exciting. In those days, it still had something to say …
	[ESME *offers the salami to* AMY *who takes the chance to put her hand on Esme's arm.*]
ESME	Amy?

DOMINIC	But now … I don't know, we're all watching video. I believe human beings have changed. They've evolved. They have different priorities.
FRANK	My goodness.
DOMINIC	The image is much more important. The image has taken the place of the word. *[FRANK nods and tries to look intelligent.]*
FRANK	Uh-huh.
DOMINIC	You know, you go to the theatre. A character comes in the door. You think, oh my God! He's going to cross the room. Jump-cut, for Christ's sake, just jump-cut! And then next thing – oh, Christ, you just know it! The bastard is going to sit down and *talk. [He shakes his head pityingly.]* And it's so slow. They do it slowly. And the way they act! It's so old-fashioned. In these big barns and they all have to shout. Why don't we admit it? It's been superseded. It had its moment, but its moment has gone. *[AMY looks nervously across at her mother, but ESME is not remotely concerned.]* Of course, I defer to you, Esme …
ESME	Thank you …
DOMINIC	You understand it all much better than me. But who does theatre reach? Who is it talking to? Obvious. To me, it's just wank time.
ESME	I see. Well, it's good that at least you've not made up your mind …
DOMINIC	Look …
ESME	No, really, that famed objectivity. He's open-minded …
AMY	*[smiles]* Yes …
ESME	Wouldn't you say? Dominic has no agenda or anything …
DOMINIC	All right, very funny …
ESME	There's no question of you boys having to work to a script! *[She seems oddly cheered as she moves round with the plates.]* Have you noticed? It's always the death of the theatre. The death of the novel. The death of poetry. The death of whatever they fancy this week. Except there's one thing it's never the death of. Somehow it's never the death of *themselves*.

Martin Crimp

From *Attempts on her Life* (1997)

Martin Crimp's play is a series of 16 scenarios in which various unspecified voices discuss Anne. It is not clear whether she was a murderer or victim or both, but in each of the scenes a powerful picture is built up. This extract is part of scenario 6, 'Mum and Dad'. A dash (–) indicates a change of speaker and / indicates where the speech overlaps.

— It's quite clear that her mind's / made up.
— It's not a cry for help. It's very important to establish that, wouldn't you agree, from the outset. It's very important to establish that no one could've helped / her at that point.
— No one could've helped her – not her Mum – not her Dad – and certainly none of her so-called / *friends*.
— She wouldn't've / wanted help.
— Help is the last thing she would've wanted.
   Silence. In the silence:

> 'She enjoys spending lots of time with guests,
> and gets a feeling of great satisfaction
> when everyone is having a good time.
> She says there are lots of hugs at the station
> when it's time to go home, with holidaymakers
> waving and calling out
> "see you next time" from the train window.'

Laughter all through next passage:
— Some of the strange things she says ...
— Some of the strange things she says to her Mum and Dad as a child: 'I feel like a screen.'
— 'I feel like a screen.'
— She's lying there, isn't she, with the tube in her poor thin arm, looking terribly pale, whiter in fact than / the *pillow*.
— 'Like a TV screen,' she says, 'where everything from the front looks real and alive, but round the back there's just dust and a few wires.'
— 'Dust and a few wires.' Her imagination ...
— She says she's not a real character like you get in a book or on TV, but a *lack* of character, an *absence* she calls it, doesn't she, of character.
— An absence of character, whatever that means ...
— Then she wants to be a terrorist, doesn't she?
— That's right. She comes down one night to the kitchen with those big earnest eyes of hers and tells her Mum and Dad she wants to be a terrorist.

- The looks on their faces ...
- She wants her own little room and a gun and a list of names.
- 'Targets.'
- A list – that's right – of so-called targets and their photographs. She wants to kill one a week then come back to the little room and drink Earl Grey tea.
- That's right – it has to be Earl Grey – and it has to be one a week.
- Her poor Mum and Dad are / horrified.
- They absolutely don't know how to take this.
- They've never bought Earl Grey tea / in their lives.
- She'd like to act like a machine, wouldn't she.
- Act? She'd like to be a machine. Sometimes she spends days on end, whole days on end, pretending to be a television / or a car.
- A car or a television, an automatic pistol or a treadle sewing-machine.
  Silence. In the silence:

  'She is an excellent singles' host,
  and loves to take people
  on guided walks.'
- A sewing machine ... The things she comes out with ...

4 | Critical approaches to 20th-century British drama

- How important are issues such as gender and class in understanding criticism and drama?

- How far does criticism reflect the time when it was written?

- How have writers and directors changed the ways in which we think about 20th-century drama?

Kinds of criticism

When you begin to think about British drama it is important to be able to assess the views of others, so that you are aware of the range of critical views and arguments, and also of the way that critics argue and how they use evidence. As a reader and a critic, you come to the study of British drama with some preconceptions and experiences which will shape your understanding, but of which you may not be aware. What sex you are, where you come from and your experience of life all influence your understanding in ways you may take for granted. The critic is always in this position. Some critics have hoped for a kind of objectivity which is able to detach personality from criticism to see the object as it really is. Many other critics have stressed how difficult, if not impossible, this is. As a result, when you read dramatic criticism you will find a wide range of perspectives. It is therefore an essential part of reading criticism to detect the critical point of view. All critics and readers have their own interests and slants on what they read, but there are some clear theoretical positions that critics may show. They will naturally focus on areas of the play that suit them and their arguments. A Marxist critic, for example, will look at issues of class and power from the standpoint of the working class. The focus will be on public and political issues. As Marxists look forward to the victory of a class revolution, Marxist theatre tends to be positive and bracing in tone. A feminist will be mainly interested in women characters, the treatment of gender or of the family. A Freudian or psychoanalytic critic will look at the ways that unconscious drives shape character and plot.

Look Back in Anger and the critics

The following extracts from criticism of *Look Back in Anger* should help you to analyse critical perspective, and to see how criticism is more like an ongoing

argument and less like the accumulation of wisdom. It is also important to notice how these critics respond to the play in the light of when they were writing and the issues of the day. It does not matter if you do not know the play.

▶ Examine the following critical extracts on *Look Back in Anger*. Note the main argument of each one and the critic's viewpoint. Which reviews seem to come from clear viewpoints such as Marxist, feminist or psychoanalytical? Which ones are most positive or negative about the play?

1

Look Back in Anger presents post-war youth as it really is, with special emphasis on the non-U intelligentsia who live in bed-sitters and divide the Sunday papers into two groups, 'posh' and 'wet'. To have done this at all would be a signal achievement; to have done it in a first play is a minor miracle. All the qualities are there, qualities one had despaired of ever seeing on the stage – the drift towards anarchy, the instinctive leftishness, the automatic rejection of 'official' attitudes, the surrealist sense of humour (Jimmy describes a pansy friend as 'a female Emily Brontë'), the casual promiscuity, the sense of lacking a crusade worth fighting for and, underlying all these, the determination that no-one who dies shall go unmourned.

One cannot imagine Jimmy Porter listening with a straight face to speeches about our inalienable right to flog Cypriot schoolboys. You could never mobilise him and his kind into a lynching mob, since the art he lives for, jazz, was invented by Negroes; and if you gave him a razor, he would do nothing with it but shave. The Porters of our time deplore the tyranny of 'good taste' and refuse to accept 'emotional' as a term of abuse; they are classless, and they are also leaderless … I doubt if I could love anyone who did not wish to see *Look Back in Anger*. It is the best young play of its decade.

(Kenneth Tynan in the *Observer*, 1956)

▶ This is a review that helped to ensure the success of the play. What is the attitude of the critic and what evidence would you use to demonstrate it?

2

Superbly acted by its cast of five, this play by 27-year-old actor-turned-author John Osborne starts rich in promise, but lets us down with a sickening melodramatic thud.

Conceived as a protest against the smug middle-class morality reflected in most West End plays, it is set in a squalid one-roomed flat in a Midlands town – the kind of play Tennessee Williams might have written if he had spent a month of rainy Sundays in Birmingham. A young man, cynical, neurotic, of working-class stock, lashes his middle-class wife from one indignity to another. We laugh at some of his cynical jokes, but can feel no sympathy – not even pity – for a character who becomes almost as tiresome with his bitter pronouncements as the people he despises.

Mr. Osborne's dialogue is fluent, often very funny (a chinless wonder from Sandhurst is described as 'a platitude from outer space'). He does indeed look back in anger. But his development as a writer will depend upon what he looks forward to.

(P.G. in *The Daily Worker*, 1956)

▶ Examine how this reviewer treats the issue of class. What does he see as the play's main weakness? How does answering these questions lead you to understand the reviewer's Marxist perspective?

3

It was in its attitudes to the sanctities of class and sex that the play was felt to be most sensational. It's hard to say now which was more shocking: that the heroine should be seen on stage in her petticoat (not a Noel Coward style negligée), or that she was doing the ironing while wearing it. Censorship in the public theatres had effectively banned the airing, not just of sexual issues, but of religious and political topics too. Yet ... what may then have looked very advanced was really very reactionary. The fifties were characterised by a deep misogyny which was to necessitate the re-emergence of feminism in the sixties. What was happening was a kind of forcible repatriation of women once the war that had allowed them to take a wide range of unaccustomed roles was over and the men returned to take up the places that were traditionally theirs. The chauvinism of *Look Back in Anger* went unremarked at the time, of course.

(Cecily Palser Havely *Literature in the Modern World*, 1991)

▶ What is the central image of the play for Cecily Palser Havely and how does this relate to the critic's viewpoint? In what ways is her position a feminist one? How does she relate the play to wider social and historical issues?

4

Well, guess what? A new production for the National by Gregory Hersov suggests that the play will, after all, survive into the millennium, that it does still have something to say to us, ... Jimmy's rootless rage, his sense of impending doom, his regret for a past he never knew, all somehow seem very 1990s. Jimmy is a man behaving badly, and the ultimate irony has always been that it was never with him that Osborne identified; the only character in the entire script written with love and sympathy and respect has always been the confused old colonel whom Osborne ultimately became himself in real life.

By busting the play down to two acts, by facing the distinct possibility that Jimmy is as much in love with his room-mate Cliff as with either of the women who try in very different ways to tame him, and by turning a once *dangerously* sentimental ending into something chilly as Strindberg, Hersov has shot thousands of volts through the text and made it as relevant, topical, angry and intriguing as it has never been since those first heady days at the Court.

(Sheridan Morley in *The Spectator*, 24 July 1999)

▶ What does Morley see as surprising about the play? How does he suggest that this production makes the play relevant to the 1990s and revives the impact of the first production?

5

At base Sheen's Jimmy is not the fiery opponent of British conservatism he likes to believe himself. For all his attacks on his wife's supposed failure to match him for emotional vitality he is not exactly the frustrated D.H. Lawrence that Kenneth Branagh suggested when he played the role in 1989. There is something oddly insecure about Sheen's Cockney-accented exhibitionism, swagger and trademark grin. More than any Jimmy I've seen, he shows why a graduate is squandering his intellect and energy running a sweet stall in a provincial market.

Lines about Jimmy's futility, his bashfulness when he meets Alison, his helpless sorrow at his father's premature death, all fall into place. When he makes a dive for Alison's lap, you begin to sense that his misogyny conceals a craving for the good mother neither he nor Osborne had. Even the famous 'there are no good, brave causes left' has the whiff of personal inadequacy. The unsentimental suggestion is that he is rootless and more than a bit lost.

(Benedict Nightingale in *The Times*, 17 July 1999)

▶ What does Benedict Nightingale see as the core of the play and how does this affect a political reading of *Look Back in Anger*?

6

It now seems incredible that it was once thought of as a political play;
incredible that intelligent people could have been taken in by the
occasional thump of bullying rhetoric ('no more good brave causes',
and so on) into supposing that Jimmy Porter was a representative
hero, or that he cared for anyone but himself. ...

But Jimmy's anger, critically celebrated by Osborne (despite a few
sops thrown to the other characters), now makes him look positively
creepy. It is an instrument of domination – like his trumpet, only more
so – and he himself is a menace of a not unfamiliar type, one of those
little Hitlers who have to settle for finding their victims in their
immediate circle.

(John Gross in the Sunday Telegraph, 18 July 1999)

▶ Compare and contrast this review with Kenneth Tynan's.

7

Nobody understood the weight of history that bears down on John
Osborne's *Look Back in Anger* ... better than Osborne himself. In his
introduction to Faber's collected edition of his plays, published the
year before he died in 1994, he described himself as 'buried' by the
play's reputation, 'mystified by the myth'. Hersov clearly feels
oppressed by history, too, for he has tried to take this iconic text in a
different direction, away from the class politics that shaped its
original reception towards a sexual politics with which we are more
familiar.

Yet history follows you even as you try to escape it. The myth of
The Angry Young Man, that felicitous phrase of a Royal Court press
officer in May 1956, cannot be entirely separated from the play, even
if the historical event with which it is most closely associated,
Britain's humiliating attempt to reassert her lost imperial authority by
invading Egypt, didn't happen till six months after the opening night.
When Kenneth Tynan in his review described Osborne as 'the first
spokesman in the London theatre' for a new post-war generation he
was absolutely right. The fierce and vivid language of the play, its
dingy attic setting in a Midlands town, were so unfamiliar to the
prevailing theatrical establishment that on its first night, according to
Osborne, the audience was 'adrift, like Eskimos watching a
Restoration comedy'.

It was Osborne's articulation of a new voice – classless according
to Tynan, but in fact aggressively lower-middle class, a product of the
Welfare State and the 1944 Education Act that sent his anti-hero to a

'white-tile' university – that helped to effect the theatrical revolution that followed. Excepting its language, a profoundly conventional one-set, three-act, small-cast drama managed to break the conventions that kept the classes in their places as neatly as the architecture of Edwardian West End theatres separated the wealthy in the stalls from the poor in the gallery.

(Robert Hewison in *The Sunday Times*, 25 July 1999)

▶ How does Robert Hewison place the play in a historical context to bring out its significance today?

▶ Using three or four of the extracts above, compare the critical responses between 1956 and 1999, and show how these responses have developed.

Different critical viewpoints

In Willy Russell's *Educating Rita* (1978), Frank is a university teacher and Rita, a hairdresser, is his adult pupil. The following extract expresses a disagreement about what criticism should be.

FRANK	Now the piece you wrote for me on – what was it called …?
RITA	… *Rubyfruit Jungle*.
FRANK	Yes, it was – erm …
RITA	Crap?
FRANK	No. Erm – the thing is, it was an appreciation, a descriptive piece. What you have to learn is criticism.
RITA	What's the difference? …
FRANK	Well. You must try to remember that criticism is purely objective. It should be approached almost as a science. It must be supported by reference to established literary critique. Criticism is never subjective and should not be confused with partisan interpretation. In criticism sentiment has no place. *[He picks up the copy of* Howards End.*]* Tell me, what did you think of *Howards End*?
RITA	It was crap.
FRANK	What?
RITA	I thought it was crap!
FRANK	Crap? And who are you citing in support of your thesis, F.R. Leavis?
RITA	No. Me!

FRANK	What have I just said? 'Me' is subjective.
RITA	Well it's what I think.

▶ Who do you think is right in this exchange? Discuss what you think are the main points in favour of Frank and Rita's positions and their main weaknesses.

Frank supports his view about the objectivity of criticism by implying that there is a body of agreed wisdom, but, as the debate on *Look Back in Anger* illustrated, this is often not the way that criticism works.

How can the reader deal with critics who are at odds with each other? Take, for example, the way that the critics Martin Esslin and Simon Trussler discuss Pinter's *The Homecoming*, a play which has been the subject of considerable critical comment.

▶ Read the views of the two critics which follow (and also the extract from the play in Part 3, pages 83–84) and note down your first impressions.

It is my conviction that *The Homecoming*, while being a poetic image of a basic human situation, can also stand up to the most meticulous examination as a piece of realistic theatre, and that, indeed, its achievement is the perfect fusion of extreme realism with the quality of an archetypal dream image of wish-fulfilment …

At the end of the play Ruth rules the household. This is the 'homecoming' of the title … the mother whom the son desires in his infancy at the moment of the first awakening of his sexuality, is not an old woman but a young one. It is her image which still dominates his dreams when he is grown up. Ruth, the mother of three boys whose ages must range from five to three, therefore represents the dreams of Lenny and Joey in that period of their lives. The final image of *The Homecoming* therefore is the culmination of their Oedipal dreams: their mother, young and beautiful, has become available to them as a sexual partner, as a 'whore', while the defeated father grovels on the floor pleading for some sexual favours. This wish-fulfilment dream is the exact reversal of the real situation that faces a young son: the father in proud possession and the son rejected, oppressed, dominated.

(Martin Esslin *Pinter the Playwright*, 1982)

So Esslin sees the play in two ways: on one hand, it can be taken as a piece of 'realist theatre' with recognisable characters and a coherent plot, and on the other it is a dreamlike myth. (Oedipus slept with his mother and killed his father:

Sigmund Freud suggested the idea of the Oedipus complex as an underlying pattern of men's desires.)

▶ Which of these accorded more with your first impressions? Can plays work on two such different levels?

The critic Simon Trussler saw the play differently. He wrote about Max:

> His role gets considerable dramatic emphasis – it is with an impression of Max that the play both begins and ends. Yet … his grand climacteric is one of the uneasiest scenes in a play full of uneasy scenes, as falling on his knees, whimpering and moaning, he crawls past the prone body of his brother and approaches Ruth:
> I'm not an old man
> *[He looks up at her.]*
> Do you hear me?
> *[He raises his face to her.]*
> Kiss me.
> *[She continues to touch Joey's head, lightly. Lenny stands, watching.]*
> And the curtain falls. Again, the sheer grotesqueness of it all engages the attention – but only instantaneously, and without connecting the scene to what has gone before, let alone to any conceivable reality outside the play itself. In between times, Max has merely been benevolent or bellicose, affectionate or aggressive, clever or thick-headed – yet always one senses as it suits Pinter's purpose, not Max's mood …
> *The Homecoming* is in short a modishly intellectualised melodrama, its violence modulated by its vagueness, its emotional stereotyping disguised by carefully planted oddities of juxtaposition and expression. To suspend disbelief in this play is to call a temporary halt to one's humanity.
> (Simon Trussler *The Plays of Harold Pinter*, 1973)

Here the critics disagree not only about the nature of the work, but also about its fundamental value.

▶ What are Trussler's main objections to this scene? By implication what constitutes (for him) good serious drama? You might find it helpful to think about the word 'melodrama' and how Trussler uses it in this passage. Notice how for Esslin the play reached towards myth and universal significance, whereas for Trussler the false surface and melodramatic trickery are all.

How can the student begin to deal with such a radical difference of critical views? The first thing is to go back to the text and, by looking closely at it, examine and test the critical views. Look closely at Max's collapse. Can you believe in him as a character here, or is Pinter merely playing on the audience's emotions? In the extract, the first part is addressed to Lenny and the final words to Ruth. Has Max failed to get the response he wanted from his son, and therefore turned in hope or despair to his last chance, Ruth? And, crucially, what do you make of his last words, 'Kiss me'? You might notice too the final stage directions as Ruth continues to touch Joey's hair lightly (like a mother or a lover?) and Lenny watches in (powerful?) silence. There is a stage tableau here and the positioning of the figures might well suggest their status and power.

Three critics: Brecht, Brook and Edgar

Sometimes criticism can be important because it defines a dramatic style and becomes an important influence on productions and thought about the theatre. The following extracts have been chosen to illustrate the way in which playwrights and directors who are also critics have defined and helped to shape the theatre of their day.

Brecht's epic theatre

Brecht drew a famous distinction between the old type of theatre, based on Greek tragedy, and his own practice, based on Shakespeare. He stressed, however, that this was a not a distinction of *kind* but rather a distinction of *emphasis*.

▶ Read Brecht's distinction between 'epic theatre' and 'dramatic theatre' opposite. After a first reading, make brief notes on what you think are the major differences. Which plays or parts of plays that you have read seem to owe most to Brecht? Which plays the least?

> The modern theatre is the epic theatre. The following table shows certain changes of emphasis as between the dramatic and epic theatre.

Dramatic theatre	Epic theatre
Plot	Narrative
Implicates the spectator in a stage situation	Turns the spectator into an observer but ...
Wears down his capacity for action	Arouses his capacity for action
Provides him with sensations	Forces him to take decisions
Experience	Picture of the world
The spectator is involved in something	He is made to face something
Suggestion	Argument
Instinctive feelings are preserved	Brought to the point of recognition
The spectator is in the thick of it, shares the experience	The spectator stands outside, studies
The human being is taken for granted	The human being is the object of the enquiry
He is unalterable	He is alterable and able to alter
Eyes on the finish	Eyes on the course
One scene makes another	Each scene for itself
Growth	Montage
Linear development	In curves
Evolutionary determinism	Jumps
Man as a fixed point	Man as a process
Thought determines being	Social being determines thought
Feeling	Reason

(*Brecht on Theatre*, 1964)

Brook's 'empty space'

The director and writer, Peter Brook, published *The Empty Space* in 1968 and it has since become a classic of writing about the theatre. Read the following extract:

I can take any empty space and call it a bare stage. A man walks across this empty space whilst someone else is watching him and this is all that is needed for an act of theatre to be engaged. Yet when we talk about theatre this is not quite what we mean. Red curtains, spotlights, blank verse, laughter, darkness, these are all confusedly superimposed in a messy image covered by one all-purpose word. We talk of the cinema killing the theatre, and in that phrase we refer to the theatre as it was when the cinema was born, a theatre of box office, foyer, tip-up seats, footlights, scene changes, intervals, music, as though the theatre was by definition these and little more.

Brook goes on to split the word theatre into four different categories: Deadly Theatre, Holy Theatre, Rough Theatre and Immediate Theatre.

It is always the popular theatre that saves the day. Through the ages it has taken many forms, and there is only one factor that they all have in common – a roughness. Salt, sweat, noise, smell: the theatre that's not in a theatre, the theatre on carts, on wagons, on trestles, audiences standing, drinking, sitting round tables, audiences joining in, answering back; theatre in back rooms, upstairs rooms, barns; the one-night stands, the torn sheet pinned up across the hall, the battered screen to cover the quick changes – that one generic term, theatre covers all this and the sparkling chandeliers too …

▶ How helpful do you find Brook's ideas of a bare stage as the basis of all theatre?

▶ What contrasting ideas of theatre does Brook outline here?

▶ What elements of 'popular theatre' are relevant to the plays you have read?

Edgar: the future of drama?

David Edgar believes that writers are beginning to reject simple ideas of plot and character, or at least to think about dramatic form in new ways. He uses Martin Crimp's play, *Some Attempts on her Life* (Part 3, pages 96–97), as an example:

A series of apparently disconnected groups and individuals describe what we are invited to think of as a single woman called Anne, possessed nonetheless of various nationalities, histories and ages, who appears at one point to be a terrorist (of left or right), and at another the drowned daughter of grieving parents, at another an artist and even a newly launched car. Crimp's purpose is not only to question whether we can truly know another human being, but whether we can regard other people as existing at all independent of the models we construct of them. And he does this not by bald statement, but by playing an elaborate and sophisticated game with the audience's expectations of how scenes connect with narrative.
    So it may be that precisely at the moment when television, radio and film drama are rushing pell-mell back towards the certainties of

traditional genre-based narrative forms, new British playwrights are
finding ways to challenge the assumptions of traditional storytelling ...

(*State of Play* ed. David Edgar, 1999)

▶ How does this critic help you to understand the extract?

▶ Why do some modern playwrights and critics find traditional approaches to plot
and character unsatisfactory?

▶ Compare and contrast the different kinds of drama that these three critics are
interested in.

Assignments

1 Read the play reviews in the newspapers. Has one critic and/or one
   newspaper a particular bias or slant in its reviews? Try to find several
   reviews of the same production and compare and contrast them.

2 Read two or three critics of a play you know well and note their
   viewpoints and where they differ. Now discuss how far you agree with
   each view and argue your own.

3 How might a Marxist or a feminist critic view the extract from *Hindle
   Wakes* (Part 3, pages 72–74)? Write a one-paragraph review from each
   perspective and compare the results. Now take a play you know well and
   write a paragraph about it from a theoretical point of view. How far did
   you wish to challenge this paragraph from your own point of view?

4 'Closure' is the critical term used to describe the way a writer brings his
   work to an end. 'Closed' endings give an impression of completeness or
   finality: comedies end in marriage, tragedies in death. Most modern
   dramatists have preferred 'open' endings, leaving the audience in
   suspense. Look in detail at the extract from the end of *Hobson's Choice*
   and compare it with the ending of *The Homecoming* (Part 3, pages 74–76
   and pages 83–84).
   'Most plays new end pessimistically. The hero does not get the loot or
   the girl ...' wrote the director and critic Max Stafford-Clark in 1990. With
   these critical remarks about closure in mind, compare the ending of a
   play you are studying with one of the extracts.

5 | How to write about 20th-century British drama

Using criticism

Writing about drama demands the same kinds of understanding and skills as writing about novels or poetry. The first necessity is to get to know the text you are reading extremely well. The second is to read around the text. This may mean reading other works by the same writer, and supplementing that reading with relevant criticism. You should read criticism, but be aware of the danger of relying too heavily or too closely on professional critics. If you are able to engage with critics, question what they are saying and disagree when appropriate, then your writing will be much strengthened.

Use criticism:

- to be aware of the issues and themes that have been discussed
- to focus on the central issues which critics disagree about
- to try to formulate your own views of the works you are reading.

The importance of a considered personal response must be stressed. If you can develop the habit of using criticism as a stimulus to your own ideas, it will prove invaluable to your work.

Writing about drama

Writing about drama does have some distinctive features that come from the nature of drama itself. If you are writing about a poem or a novel, you are writing about the thing itself: the novelist or the poet had you, the reader, in mind as he or she wrote. When you read a play, however, you are not judging the finished product, for plays are, with very few exceptions, written to be performed. In this sense then, you may feel that you are studying a shadow of a work of art rather than the real thing.

There are problems here for every student of drama, but they can be surmounted in many different ways. The most obvious and best way is to see a production of the texts you are reading, and/or of other works of the same writer or period. With the reading that you have done, you will now be able to place the play in a dramatic context. Seeing a production is, of course, not always possible, but there are many other ways of moving the play out of the study. There are some excellent videos available of many modern texts. (See Part 6: Resources, page 121.)

Glossary

Absurdist drama theatre that presents the world as unknowable, random and unpredictable. *Waiting for Godot* is the classic statement of this predicament. Tom Stoppard's *Rosencrantz and Guildenstern* and Pinter's *The Birthday Party* show how different are the products of the theatre of the absurd.

Agit-prop a contraction of 'agitational propaganda'. A style of drama that has a clear political or social message and aims to convert its audience. In Britain this is the style of the Workers' Theatre of the 1930s and the early work of Brenton, Edgar and Barker.

Black comedy comedy that deals with disturbing issues and tends to unsettle and question rather than simply to entertain. Joe Orton's *Loot* is a good example.

Catharsis an idea going back to the ancient Greek philosopher, Aristotle, that tragedy should give the audience a kind of emotional release or purging.

Comedy of manners a type of comedy that treats wittily the manners and morals of society.

Community theatre theatre whose subject is the 'everyday suffering of people's lives', often performed in places where people gather to socialise, dealing with local and community issues and using local people as actors.

Epic theatre this form of theatre was developed and popularised by Brecht. It was defined by Brecht himself by contrast with the tragic mode (see pages 106–107). During the 1970s and 1980s it became a dominant style of British drama in the work of Bond, Edgar, Hare and Brenton.

Farce comedy that relies on fast pace, physical action and stereotypical characters. Ayckbourn's *Bedroom Farce* and Orton's *What the Butler Saw* are clear examples. Farce is often an element of other kinds of comedy.

Fourth wall naturalism if the stage is imagined as a room, the fourth wall has been cut away to allow the audience to see straight through.

Genre a kind of representation, as for example, tragedy.

Acting out the scenes with fellow students or friends is particularly helpful. If you are working in small groups, you might pick out a scene that you have different views about and present it in two or three different interpretations, and then discuss the differences between them. Even if all these approaches are impracticable, always bear in mind as you are reading that you are reading a *play*. As you read, you should be directing an imaginary production in your head.

▶ Choose a brief scene from a play that you are reading and write a 'Director's notebook'. State what you feel is central to the scene and, in detail, how you would use all the resources of the stage to express your vision.

Developing a sense of dramatic genre

It is helpful to develop a sense of dramatic genre so that you can begin to understand the kind of theatre to which a work may belong. This will help you to bring the right kind of focus to a play. That is not to say that these categories help you to pigeon-hole theatre, rather the reverse: they should enable you to see the ways in which a play can belong to a genre and then change into something else; or perhaps elude classification completely!

▶ Bear in mind the following categories (you might use the glossary to help you to define them): tragedy; the well-made play; naturalism; farce; poetic drama; realism; melodrama; the theatre of the absurd; kitchen sink drama.

Read the following extract. Which category or categories might help you to place it?

The extract is taken from *Lear* (1972) by Edward Bond, who based the play on Shakespeare's tragedy, *King Lear*. The blinded old King Lear has taken refuge in the country; Thomas and Susan have a small farm with pigs. The ghost is that of the young farmer who had lived there before he was slaughtered by soldiers and buried. News has just arrived that soldiers are in the village looking for Lear.

LEAR	Listen, I must talk to you. I'm going on a journey and Susan will lead me.
THOMAS	Yes, go into hiding! Don't let them get their filthy hands on you.
LEAR	Tomorrow morning we'll get up and have breakfast together and you'll go to work, but Susan will stay with me. She may not be back tomorrow evening, but she'll be back soon I promise you. You're fond of me and I've been happy with you. I'm lucky. Now I have only one more wish – to live till I'm much older and become as cunning as the fox, who knows how to live. *Then* I could teach you.

<table>
<tr><td></td><td colspan="2">Off, distant squealing of angry pigs further off than at the end of Act One, Scene Seven.</td></tr>
<tr><td>THOMAS</td><td>The pigs!</td></tr>
<tr><td>SUSAN</td><td>What is it?</td></tr>
<tr><td></td><td>SUSAN and THOMAS run off. LEAR stands by himself.</td></tr>
<tr><td>THOMAS</td><td>[off] They've gone mad.</td></tr>
<tr><td>SUSAN</td><td>[off] Quick!</td></tr>
<tr><td>THOMAS</td><td>[off] That way!</td></tr>
<tr><td>SUSAN</td><td>[off] Look out!</td></tr>
<tr><td>THOMAS</td><td>[off] Berserk! Wup-wup-wup-wup-wup-wup-wup!</td></tr>
<tr><td>SUSAN</td><td>[off] Wup-wup-wup! Mad!</td></tr>
<tr><td></td><td>The GHOST stumbles in. It is covered with blood. The pig squeals slowly die out. A few more isolated calls of 'wup'.</td></tr>
<tr><td>GHOST</td><td>The pigs! I'm torn! They gored me! Help me, help me! I'll die!</td></tr>
<tr><td>LEAR</td><td>[holds him] I can't.</td></tr>
<tr><td>GHOST</td><td>Lear! Hold me!</td></tr>
<tr><td>LEAR</td><td>No, too late! It's far too late! You were killed long ago! You must die! I love you, I'll always remember you, but I can't help you. Die, for your own sake die!</td></tr>
<tr><td>GHOST</td><td>O Lear, I am dead!</td></tr>
<tr><td></td><td>The GHOST's head falls back. It is dead. It drops at LEAR's feet. The calls and pig squeals stop.</td></tr>
<tr><td>LEAR</td><td>I see my life, a black tree by a pool. The branches are covered with tears. The tears are shining with light. The wind blows the tears in the sky. And my tears fall down on me.</td></tr>
</table>

It is of course hard to judge an extract, especially from a dramatist whose first plays met with critical incomprehension. When reading an extract like this, you have to ask yourself: how could it be performed on stage, and the related question: what sort of play is this? In the background is one of Shakespeare's greatest tragedies, *King Lear*, but how far, if at all, are you aware of it here? The extract opens with some dialogue that appears flatly naturalistic, but does it have any further depth? You might notice two phrases: 'I'm going on a journey,' and 'as cunning as the fox'. What do they suggest to you? Is Lear's language here of the kind you might expect from a king? How do you visualise in your imaginary production the next part with the pigs offstage? Is it comic? Or frightening? What should Lear be doing as he is left alone on stage? When the Ghost enters, gored by the pigs he used to tend, Lear says to him that he cannot be saved, as he is long dead. Is this logical absurdity, or black comedy, or even tragic pity?

In the final speech there is a dramatic switch to another style. Here Lear uses much more poetic language and images that might remind you of the highly compressed Japanese lyric verse form called *haiku*. Notice the contrast with the preceding speeches and the action. What does this make you feel for Lear himself?

Dealing with this difficult passage should help you to understand two vital points: first, that an understanding of a dramatic text can only come from a close examination of the words themselves, and, second, that the words are part of an overall dramatic action and make limited sense without it.

▶ Having worked through the text and considered the questions above, what category or categories of theatre do you think are most useful to describe this extract? Have you changed/modified your views since completing the task on page 111?

There are a number of possible responses to the extract from *Lear* that may include poetic drama, the theatre of cruelty, the theatre of the absurd, even tragedy. A full understanding only comes when you are alert to the switches of mood and style, and when you develop awareness that playwrights of today rarely use a single dramatic genre, but tend to move from one to another to achieve their aims. This lack of a settled genre often makes an audience more uncertain about the response it should give to much modern drama: an audience watching a play by Pinter, for example, is often divided between those who laugh and those who find his plays deeply disturbing. The best approaches will often come through exploring rather than avoiding the complexity of modern drama. Use your own puzzlement or questions as the starting point for exploration of the plays you are reading and be open to possibilities and different readings.

Discussing context

The word 'context' derives from the Latin verb *contexere*, meaning 'to weave'. Hence a context is something woven from different strands. This idea of weaving together strands to produce a fabric is a good image for a writer dealing with his or her different materials.

The starting point in discussing context is best seen as *within the text itself*, not outside it. In this way, the text will inform the reader which contexts are relevant and illuminating. Or, to put it another way, every reader will shape the text in the light of his or her distinctive reading by choosing which contextual lenses to use.

▶ Consider the extract from Edward Bond's *Saved* (Part 3, pages 84–86) and write down four or five contexts that might be discussed.

Which of these contexts do you think sheds most light on the extract?

The simplest approach is to start from the text and to work outwards. Contexts emerge from the language of the play. The violence and hatred that are Bond's theme are present throughout ('Piss on it! Piss on it!'). The crudeness of the vocabulary and the flatness of the language express the mean and deprived lives of these men. There is a London context here too, with references to Guy Fawkes and a fair on Hampstead Heath, and a social context with repeated references to the park where killing becomes a recreation. The breakdown of the traditional family is also relevant: 'the sing-song' voice at the end is that of the lone parent bringing up her child ('Muggins 'ere'). So, by examining the language in detail, the play's different contexts begin to emerge.

There are many other ways to develop the issues of context here. For example, what is the extract's *dramatic* context? The first approach is to see the extract as part of a larger whole, the play itself. Why did Bond place this moment at the exact centre of his play and how does it relate to the whole of *Saved*? The second might be to relate it more specifically to a performance, discussing, for example, its use of dramatic devices: the two sounds here of 'buzzing' and the ringing of the bell. What associations might these have?

Working outwards from the text, *Saved* could be placed in the context of other plays by Bond, through comparison and contrast. The context of genre could also be applied to the extract to discuss the ways in which Bond both uses and modifies naturalism. Or, the play could be examined as part of the programme of the Royal Court to reflect contemporary issues. All these are *dramatic* contexts and it is up to the reader, the audience and the critic to see which are the most illuminating.

The broadest contexts of all are those of the historical, social and cultural. It is helpful to know that *Saved* is a product of the mid-1960s. Thirteen years of Conservative government ended with the election victory of Harold Wilson's Labour Party in 1964. Those who had elected Labour hoped for a fairer, better-educated society. Teenage violence had been an issue since the fights of mods and rockers at Brighton in the early 1960s, and the film of Anthony Burgess' novel of youth violence, *A Clockwork Orange* (1962), had been withdrawn for fear of provoking more. The task of the socially minded critic is to show how these historical and social contexts are relevant to *Saved*. How does Bond use what the critic Stephen Greenblatt called the 'social electricity' of the issues of an underclass and of teenage violence in this play?

It must be added that each writer creates his own context. The student of Tom Stoppard's *Rosencrantz and Guildenstern*, which appeared one year after *Saved* in 1966, will find that the play's immediate context is Shakespeare's *Hamlet*, not the events of the 1960s, and that another relevant context is Beckett's *Waiting for Godot*. (The relationship that one book has with another is known as *intertextuality*.) However, Stoppard's choice of seeing the action of *Hamlet* through the eyes of two attendant lords makes its own comment on the world of princes, kings and power politics and so a social context is also relevant.

▶ Choose an extract from Part 3 and place it within its context(s). You may find it helpful to write out significant phrases and words from the extract and comment on how they point towards a context. Do you need any further reading to help you? If so, of what kind?

Comparative study

When writing about literature at advanced level you will often be asked to compare texts. There are two reasons for this. A comparison underlies any statement such as 'Pinter's plays are centrally concerned with violence'. Comparison points to similarity and enables the critic to make general points about a writer, a genre or a period. However, the use of comparison is not only to point out common ground, it is also to sharpen the sense of what is different or distinctive about an individual playwright or play. Comparison is of course not an end in itself: its purpose is to reveal more about the works under examination. The effective use of relevant and revealing comparison is often a mark of good criticism.

▶ Using the first two extracts in Part 3 and the extract from *Top Girls* (pages 72–76, and pages 88–90) compare the dramatic treatments of women.

You might find it helpful to compare the idea of the 'strong woman' in all three extracts. What qualities does she possess? Notice how marriage, class and family are treated in each. Which of the first two extracts comes to the more conventional ending and why? If marriage is important to the first two extracts, what is the focus of *Top Girls*? How does Churchill's use of an all-female cast and overlapping dialogue contribute to the effect and contrast with the other two?

In answering these questions you will naturally be noting common features (marriage, comic endings, successful women, etc.), but you will also have noted important differences and shown how comparison can enhance your critical writing. Always remember here that an effective comparison is specific and detailed.

When writing about British drama, you are not a historian seeing drama as a reflection of historical events: you should write as a critic seeing how dramatists have responded to historical and cultural electricity and have created plays from it. Which contexts you choose as most relevant and illuminating will help you to your own interpretation of the text. It is important to note that there is no one right view here: different kinds of critical approaches may highlight different areas of the text and yield contrasting but equally valid meanings. Critics will naturally focus on different key issues. There is no final right answer to the question: what is this play about? Indeed, many modern critical approaches stress the active role of the reader who will bring his or her own interpretation of the text to create meaning.

What writers, readers and audiences engage in is a dialogue with the text. If you can argue for your own interpretation, and can show understanding of the different contexts in which plays can be read, then your engagement with, and enjoyment of, British drama will be enhanced.

Assignments

1 Look at the following theatre designs. The first is of a proscenium arch stage, the second of a traverse stage, the third of a thrust stage and the fourth is of a theatre in the round.

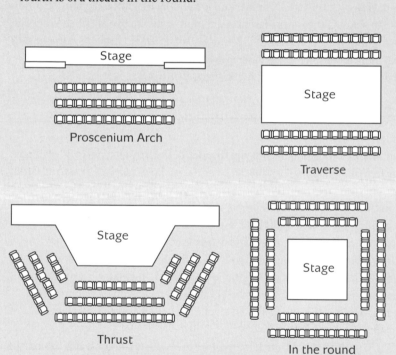

- What relationship of the actors to the audience does each form of staging encourage?
- What kind or kinds of theatre seem most appropriate for each stage?
- What form of staging would be most appropriate for the plays you are studying and why?

2　Many plays are now available on video. Find one based on a play you know and note the changes that have been made to adapt the play to the screen. The plot may have been simplified, lines cut or endings changed. Compare the play and the film. How effective was the video/screen version in conveying the original play?

3　In *The Sunday Times* Harold Hobson wrote in a review of *Serjeant Musgrave's Dance*: 'Another frightful ordeal. It is time someone reminded our advanced dramatists of the aim to give pleasure ... not to make men better, but to render them harmlessly happy.' (25 October 1959). Use examples from Part 3 and your own reading to examine how far you agree with this statement.

4　Explore some of the ways in which 20th-century British dramatists have dealt with the theme of class.

5　By examining relevant extracts in Part 3 and using your own reading, discuss what you think the term 'feminist theatre' might mean and how useful a term it is.

6　'From a critic's point of view, the history of 20th-century drama is the history of a collapsing vocabulary. Categories that were formerly thought sacred and separate begin to melt and flow together like images in a dream ...' (Kenneth Tynan).

　　Choose a scene from a play that you have read and analyse it in the light of these remarks. (You may find it helpful to reread 'Developing a sense of dramatic genre' on pages 111–113.)

7　'The only thing that binds us together is a profound unease, and laughter is the language of that unease.'(Howard Brenton) Compare and contrast any comedies you have read in the light of this statement.

8　By examining in detail any extracts from Part 3 and any plays that you have read, show how an understanding of context enhances your understanding of 20th-century British drama.

9　By examining one extract and one or more play that you have read, compare and contrast the way in which each comments on British society.

10 If you were to direct one 20th-century British drama, which one would you choose and why? What instructions would you give to the cast and to the stage and lighting designers? Choose a key moment from the play and show in detail how it should be produced on stage.

11 'Words can *only* be tested by being spoken. *Ideas* can only be worked out in real situations … the theatre is the best court society has.' (David Hare) How useful do you find this remark in discussing the plays you have read?

12 Several of the extracts are about theatre itself. Compare and contrast the attitudes they show to theatre and how these attitudes are expressed dramatically.

13 In a world of cinema, multiple television channels, videos and the Internet, what is the role of the theatre?

6 | Resources

Further reading

Texts
The *Methuen Contemporary Dramatists* series is especially convenient as it combines four or five texts within the same volume and covers most of the major dramatists.

General reference
Martin Banham *Cambridge Guide to Theatre* (Cambridge University Press, 1995)
Indispensable reference book.

J.A. Cuddon *The Penguin Dictionary of Literary Terms and Literary Theory* (Penguin, 1998)
Comprehensive and clear.

Critical series
There are three series that are very helpful. *Macmillan Modern Dramatists* provide short and clear accounts of individual playwrights, including volumes on Ayckbourn, Orton, Shaw and Stoppard. The series also includes introductions to feminist drama and British political theatre. Macmillan also publish the *Writer-Files* series (edited by Simon Trussler) which contains a detailed checklist of each writer's plays and selected criticism, and covers most of the significant British dramatists. The *Casebook* series (Macmillan) includes many detailed critical articles, but is limited to particular volumes on Osborne, Pinter, Stoppard and feminist drama.

Criticism
Jean Chothia *English Drama of the Early Modern Period 1890–1940* (Longman, 1996)
A lucid and perceptive survey relating the drama to its context and giving close reading of individual texts.

Ian Clarke *Edwardian Drama* (Faber, 1989)
Brief accounts of major dramatists and their contexts.

Richard Eyre and Nicholas Wright *Changing Stages* (Bloomsbury, 2000)
An excellent guide, readable and well illustrated.

Hugh Hunt et al *The Revels History of Drama in English: Vol.VII 1880 to the Present Day* (Methuen, 1978)
Clear and readable, but finishes in 1976.

Christopher Innes *Modern British Drama 1890–1990* (Cambridge University Press, 1996)
Detailed, dense and authoritative; deals with individual dramatists with a useful chronology.

Dominic Shellard *British Theatre since the War* (Yale, 1999)

Simon Trussler *Cambridge Illustrated History of British Theatre* (Cambridge University Press, 1994)
Excellent and brief account, beautifully illustrated.

Cultural and historical

Peter Clarke *Hope and Glory: Britain 1900–1990* (Penguin, 1996)

Boris Ford *The Cambridge Cultural History*: Volumes 9 and 10 (Cambridge University Press, 1992)
Essays on the social and cultural background.

Arthur Marwick *British Society Since 1945* (Penguin, 1996) and *A History of the Modern British Isles* (Blackwell, 2000)

Brian Moynahan *The British Century: a Photographic History of the Last Hundred Years* (Random House, 1997)
Most evocative photographs and good commentary.

John Stevenson *British Society 1914–1945* (Penguin, 1984)
A very readable introduction to the period.

Video resources

This is a list of available videos that refer to works and authors cited in the text. The director's name is bracketed.

Alan Bennett *The Madness of King George* (Hytner, 1994)
Caryl Churchill *Top Girls* (Noble/Open University, 1996)
Shelagh Delaney *A Taste of Honey* (Richardson, 1961)
Joe Orton *Entertaining Mr. Sloane* (Hickox, 1970)
John Osborne *Look Back in Anger* (Scott, 1958); *The Entertainer* (Richardson, 1960)
Harold Pinter *The Birthday Party* (Friedkin, 1968)
J.B. Priestley *An Inspector Calls* (Hamilton, 1954)
Terence Rattigan *The Winslow Boy* (Mamet, 1999)
Willy Russell *Educating Rita* (Gilbert, 1983)
G.B. Shaw *Pygmalion* (Asquith, 1938)
Tom Stoppard *Rosencrantz and Guildenstern* (Stoppard, 1990)

Websites

Good starting points are:
http://vos.ucsb.edu/shuttle/english2.html

http://theatre.haifa.ac.il/links.html

Some useful individual sites are:
Caryl Churchill
http://www.cwrl.utexas.edu/~sbowen/314fall/drama/

Harold Pinter
http://www.haroldpinter.org

George Bernard Shaw
http://www.mala.bc.ca/~mcneil/tshaw.htm

Tom Stoppard
www.sff.net/people/mberry/stoppard.htp

For further information search using individual playwrights' names.

Glossary

Absurdist drama   theatre that presents the world as unknowable, random and unpredictable. *Waiting for Godot* is the classic statement of this predicament. Tom Stoppard's *Rosencrantz and Guildenstern* and Pinter's *The Birthday Party* show how different are the products of the theatre of the absurd.

Agit-prop   a contraction of 'agitational propaganda'. A style of drama that has a clear political or social message and aims to convert its audience. In Britain this is the style of the Workers' Theatre of the 1930s and the early work of Brenton, Edgar and Barker.

Black comedy   comedy that deals with disturbing issues and tends to unsettle and question rather than simply to entertain. Joe Orton's *Loot* is a good example.

Catharsis   an idea going back to the ancient Greek philosopher, Aristotle, that tragedy should give the audience a kind of emotional release or purging.

Comedy of manners   a type of comedy that treats wittily the manners and morals of society.

Community theatre   theatre whose subject is the 'everyday suffering of people's lives', often performed in places where people gather to socialise, dealing with local and community issues and using local people as actors.

Epic theatre   this form of theatre was developed and popularised by Brecht. It was defined by Brecht himself by contrast with the tragic mode (see pages 106–107). During the 1970s and 1980s it became a dominant style of British drama in the work of Bond, Edgar, Hare and Brenton.

Farce   comedy that relies on fast pace, physical action and stereotypical characters. Ayckbourn's *Bedroom Farce* and Orton's *What the Butler Saw* are clear examples. Farce is often an element of other kinds of comedy.

Fourth wall naturalism   if the stage is imagined as a room, the fourth wall has been cut away to allow the audience to see straight through.

Genre   a kind of representation, as for example, tragedy

Kitchen sink drama   a specific kind of naturalism that customarily deals with working class domestic drama. It may be said to have started with Alison's ironing board in *Look Back in Anger*. It is the accepted style of television 'soaps'.

Living Newspaper   a documentary style of presenting current social problems and solutions. Developed in the USA in the 1930s, and much used by Workers' Theatre in Britain.

Melodrama   originating in Victorian times, melodrama is literally the mixture of drama and music. It has come to denote a theatrical genre made up from simplified characters, an exaggerated style and a predictable ending. The good are rewarded and the bad punished. The word is often used pejoratively to mean exaggerated, unreal.

Naturalism   a development from realism: a style of theatre that attempts to convey the texture of daily life with literal truthfulness.

Poetic drama   plays written in verse form. T.S. Eliot and W.H. Auden were leading exponents.

Realism   often confusingly used as synonymous with naturalism, realism attempts to convey the truth behind the appearance. It is the opposite of fantasy, but in order to reveal an underlying truth may distort everyday reality and use some form of dramatic heightening such as symbolism.

Repertory theatre   a movement of the Edwardian theatre whereby a rotation of plays allowed more experimental drama to be produced; more generally, a kind of theatre that performs plays for short runs (for example, 'weekly rep').

Sub-text   what is being said under the text; what the words really mean beneath the evasions and politeness of normal speech. Pinter is well known for his dramatic use of sub-text.

Total theatre   theatre that uses all the theatrical resources available: sound, spectacle, video, song and dance as, for example, *Oh, What a Lovely War!*

Well-made play   a play that has been so well crafted that the whole leads towards a denouement which resolves all the plot lines and issues. The name suggests the skill of the architect or the builder. Shaw, Priestley and Rattigan all used the form, which enjoyed its heyday from the 1920s to the 1950s.

Chronology

Date	Historical	Cultural	Plays
1900–09	Founding of Labour Party; death of Queen Victoria (1901): Edward VII becomes king; Women's Social and Political Union founded by Emmeline Pankhurst	Barker-Vedrenne repertory starts at the Court; Manchester Repertory Company founded	Barrie *Peter Pan*; Shaw *Man and Superman*, *Major Barbara*; Granville Barker *The Voysey Inheritance*, *Waste*, *The Madras House*; Robins *Votes for Women*; Galsworthy *Strife*
1910–19	South Wales miners' strike; George V becomes king; First World War	Workers' Theatre Movement founded	Houghton *The Younger Generation*, *Hindle Wakes*; Sowerby *Rutherford and Son*; Shaw *Pygmalion*
1920–29	First Labour government; General Strike (1926); full suffrage for women; Wall Street Crash: beginning of Great Depression	Workers' Theatre Movement refounded; first 'talkies'	Shaw *Heartbreak House*, *Saint Joan*; Coward *The Vortex*, *Hay Fever*; Corrie *In Time o' Strife*
1930–39	Unemployment reaches 2 million; Jarrow Hunger March; rise of fascism; outbreak of Spanish Civil War; George VI becomes king; beginning of Second World War	Theatre of Action (Joan Littlewood) founded; first TV broadcast	Coward *Private Lives*, *Cavalcade*; Auden *Dance of Death*, *The Ascent of F6*; Eliot *Murder in the Cathedral*; Auden and Isherwood *The Dog Beneath the Skin*
1940–49	Second World War; Labour government elected 1945: beginning of Welfare State	First Edinburgh Festival	Priestley *An Inspector Calls*; Eliot *The Cocktail Party*
1950–59	Elizabeth II becomes queen; Suez Crisis; Soviet Union invades Hungary; CND founded	*Waiting for Godot* premiers in Paris; independent TV broadcasting begins; Berliner ensemble in *Mother Courage* in London	Rattigan *The Deep Blue Sea*; Thomas *Under Milk Wood*; Osborne *Look Back in Anger*, *The Entertainer*; Wesker *Chicken Soup with Barley*, *Roots*; Pinter *The Birthday Party*; Delaney *A Taste of Honey*; Arden *Serjeant Musgrave's Dance*

1960–69	Vietnam war; student riots in Paris and London; Soviet troops march into Prague; British troops sent to Northern Ireland	Opening of National Theatre; abolition of censorship on British stage	Pinter *The Caretaker, The Homecoming, Landscape, Silence*; Wesker *Chips with Everything*; Littlewood *Oh, What a Lovely War!*; Orton *Entertaining Mr Sloane, Loot, What the Butler Saw*; Bond *Saved*; Ayckbourn *Relatively Speaking*; Stoppard *Rosencrantz and Guildenstern are Dead*; *Hair*
1970–79	Miners' Strike; 'Bloody Sunday' in Northern Ireland; Winter of Discontent'; Margaret Thatcher becomes Prime Minister; Women's Liberation Group and Gay Liberation Front founded	General Will Group Theatre founded; Joint Stock Company founded; Gay Sweatshop founded	Bond *Lear*; Brenton and Hare *Brassneck*; Churchill *Owners, A Light Shining in Buckinghamshire, Vinegar Tom, Cloud Nine*; Stoppard *Jumpers*; Ayckbourn *The Norman Conquests*; Edgar *Destiny*; Gems *Dusa, Fish, Stas and Vi, Piaf*; Hare *Plenty*
1980–89	Greenham Common Peace Camp; Falklands War; Miner's strike fails; 'Big Bang' and Black Monday on Stock Exchange; Berlin Wall falls – collapse of Eastern European communism	12 London theatres close, theatre groups disband due to funding cuts; popular musicals dominate West End	Churchill *Top Girls, Fen, Serious Money*; Stoppard *The Real Thing*; Daniels *Masterpieces*; Edgar *Maydays*; Ayckbourn *A Small Family Business*; Wertenbaker *Our Country's Good*
1990–2000	Margaret Thatcher resigns – John Major becomes Prime Minister; Gulf War; New Labour wins General Election	National Lottery funds for theatre, opera and ballet	Hare *Racing Demon, Skylight, Amy's View*; Elyot *My Night with Reg*; Kane *Blasted, Crave*; Butterworth *Mojo*; Ravenhill *Shopping and F***ing*; Marber *Closer*, Crimp *Attempts on her Life*

Index

Acknowledgements

The author and publishers wish to thank the following for permission to use copyright material:

Faber & Faber Ltd for material from David Hare *Amy's View* (1997) pp. 51–53, David Hare *Plenty* in *Plays 1* (1996) pp. 400–401; Martin Crimp *Attempts on her Life* (1997) pp. 24–26; Tom Stoppard *The Real Thing* (1982) pp. 53–54; with S.G. Phillips, Inc for John Osborne *Look Back in Anger* (1957) pp. 20–21; and with Grove/Atlantic, Inc, for Tom Stoppard *The Real Inspector Hound* (1968) pp. 15–16. Copyright © 1968 by Tom Stoppard; Harold Pinter *Landscape* (1969) pp. 29–30. Copyright © 1968 by H. Pinter Ltd; Harold Pinter *The Homecoming* (1975) pp. 80–82. Copyright © 1965, 1966 by H. Pinter Ltd; Harold Pinter *The Birthday Party* (1991) pp. 9–10. Copyright © 1959 by Harold Pinter; Samuel French Ltd for material from Harold Brighouse *Hobson's Choice* (1964) pp. 80–82; Methuen Publishing Ltd for material from Theatre Workshop *Oh, What a Lovely War!* (1965) pp. 12–15; Willy Russell *Educating Rita*, pp. 18–19; Edward Bond *Saved* (1966) pp. 69–72, Edward Bond *Lear* (1972) pp. 85–86; Caryl Churchill *Top Girls* (1982) pp. 12–13, Caryl Churchill *Fen* (1983) pp. 186–187; and Timberlake Wertenbaker *Our Country's Good* (1995) pp. 21–23; Guardian Newspapers Ltd for material from a review by Kenneth Tynan, *The Observer*, 13.5.56. Copyright © 1956 The Observer; and Kenneth Tynan 'West End Apathy', *The Observer*, 3.10.54. Copyright © 1954 *The Observer*; Random House Group Ltd for material from Arnold Wesker *Roots* in *The Wesker Trilogy*, Jonathan Cape (1960) pp. 146–148; Routledge for material from 'Their Theatre and Ours' (1932) from *Theatres of the Left 1880–1935: Workers' Theatre Movements in Britain and America* by R. Samuel, E. MacColl and S. Cosgrove; *The Spectator* for material from a review by Sheridan Morley, *The Spectator*, 24.7.99; Telegraph Group Ltd for material from a review by John Gross, *Sunday Telegraph*, 18.7.99. Copyright © Telegraph Group Ltd 1999; *Yorkshire Post* for material from Michael Hickling, 'Absolutely Farcical', Yorkshire Post, 5.5.84.

Every effort has been made to reach copyright holders; the publishers would like to hear from anyone whose rights they have unknowingly infringed.